ANGRY
PARENT
ANGRY
CHILD

Anger Management Strategies to
Stop Yelling, Keep Your Cool, and
Become A Peaceful Family

Carrie Khang

Before you begin, go grab a FREE GIFT!
Instand Printable Download- 4 pages

Pick your favorite topics or download them all. Display the poster where it is easily visible. It will help you to connect with your kids peacefully, and much more.

- Healthy Coping Skills
- Self Care Checklist
- Positive Words for Kids
- Say These Things to Your Kids Every day

Get your FREE PRINTABLES
today by scanning;

CONTENTS

INTRODUCTION

"There is no such thing as a perfect parent. So just be a real one."

– Sue Atkins

Yay! I'm having a baby!

I was so excited, jumping for joy when I saw the two lines appear on the pregnancy test strip. *This is what I've always wanted,* I thought. *I'm having a baby in a few months.*

I started fantasizing about the wonderful experiences I would have with my child. We'd walk in the park, holding hands and making conversation. I daydreamed about grocery shopping when we'd choose our favorite veggies and fruits. My child and I would enjoy the sunset while having a late afternoon picnic. Of course, I knew it wouldn't always be an easy ride; there would be struggles and plenty of hard work required. I didn't think it would be more than I could handle.

Years later, though, I have to admit: I'm not the parent I thought I would be. Raising a child is more complicated than I had imagined. I find myself failing every day. Even though I've experienced some wins, I most often failed.

You may not want to admit it to yourself or say it out loud, but parenting is **hard**. A few months after I had my son, I was scared to let anyone know that I wasn't over the moon. I didn't want anyone to see me as I was, far from being the picture-perfect mom I was supposed to be. Now, looking at the many struggles I was able to overcome, I'm glad I'm finally telling my story. I'll show you how I eventually became a peaceful parent after being an angry mom for many years.

Think of parenting this way. Do you currently own a dog or a cat? Can you still remember the first day you brought them into your home? I'm guessing you weren't an expert in taking care of these pets, but that lack of experience didn't stop you from becoming a pet owner. The reason for this is simple.

Even though you had no professional experience, you were aware of the many self-help books and blogs online where you could seek help. Through these resources, you knew you could get helpful information and advice on how to take care of your pet.

It's easy to buy a book with a title like "How to Train your Dog/Cat" and quickly become a proficient pet trainer. Sometimes in as little as a month, you begin to understand your dog or cat's body language. For example, maybe you learn that your dog whimpers when they are hungry or sense danger. This knowledge helps you to start communicating with them, and you likely feel a sense of accomplishment.

Well, that's pets.

I want you to know that the case is different when it comes to your child. You aren't raising a cat or dog but a tiny, beautiful human. You aren't a professional when it comes to matters like this. You haven't received any formal training nor have you experienced the *parenting* role before. How can you cope? How can you navigate this journey and sail peacefully through your relationship with your child?

I'm not trying to scare you, but I want to stress that you need to know the truth before embarking on this journey. Seek solutions to parenting questions *before* you need to ask them. After all, doesn't the idea of parenting sound scary enough already?

Do you think you can raise your child with just love? Of course, you can. However, I doubt that just love is enough for any child. While love is an essential part of parenting, you need to prepare yourself for this challenging journey by having a "map" that helps you navigate the turbulent sea of child-rearing.

Why I wrote this book?

I've written this book because I've been there.

I've been pushed to the point of no return, moved beyond my limit. I've lost control of my anger many times. These mishaps have caused me to fear that I'll raise an angry human.

Don't worry! I feel your frustration and disappointment. Thankfully, all hope isn't lost. Know that we can all learn from our mistakes and make amends.

By reading this book, you're already showing signs of improvement. You've realized you're on the wrong path. You know you need some help to be a better parent. That's great! I must commend you for taking this bold step.

In this book, I'll show you how to be a "Peaceful Parent." We walk through the ways to identify what makes you an angry parent and how you can become less angry. By the end of this book, you'll have an improved way of thinking, feeling, acting, and coping with common parenting problems.

How do I know reading this book will help you?

I know because I was once like you, not yet having found my escape route. I was a busy parent with a 9-to-5 job. None of my family was around for support. Because of my work, I needed to send my son to a nursery school when he was eight months old.

The situation seemed fine until my son started walking and talking. That's when the toddler years set in. When I'd pick him up from the nursery, he'd refuse to sleep or eat and throw tantrums at home. At this time, my husband and I, already exhausted from work, had already had a long day.

We were tired and sleepy. All it took was a small trigger, and soon my emotions were everywhere. What did I do? I started yelling, lashing out, and having anxiety attacks. The experience was hell for me.

I became depressed. I felt lost and broken, even beginning to regret my decision to bring a child into this world. I hated my life so much and didn't want to continue living that kind of life. I knew I needed peace so I could be happy and create good times with my bundle of joy.

Of course, there were happy moments during that time, but the bad ones overwhelmed them. So while I was grateful for having my son, I wanted more for us. I wanted to be a better parent and for my son to act according to the good standards I set. This acknowledgment set me out to seek solutions.

I researched and read a lot of parenting books. It wasn't easy at first because I resorted to the trial-and-error method. In other words, I applied what I learned to my daily life with my son to see what worked and what didn't work for us.

In the 13 years, I've spent with my son, I've learned a lot at each step of his growth. I'm passionate about sharing what I have learned. If I can become a peaceful parent after my hellish experience, you can do the same! I wish I knew the tips I share in this book before my son was born. Those initial years would have been a more beautiful experience.

I know you're an amazing person. Even though parenting is a big deal that can prove challenging, **you've got this.** With the right information and the resources available in this book, parenting will be a much smoother ride.

Remember that you are raising a tiny, adorable human, and the effort is going to be worth it. I can guarantee that.

So, are you ready to start this journey with me? I think (hope?) I got a resounding YES from you.

Buckle up, and let's go!

PART I
I AM AN ANGRY PARENT

CHAPTER 1

WHAT IS PARENTAL ANGER

"Holding onto anger is like grasping a hot coal with the intent of throwing it at someone else; you are the one who gets burned."

— Buddha

It was a Monday morning, and I'd barely rested over the weekend. I was in a rush, trying to get to work early since my boss had raised concerns about my frequent lateness. As I cooked breakfast in the kitchen, I felt like I was racing against time.

Suddenly, I heard a loud wail echo through the house. I rushed to my son's room and saw him on the floor with clothes everywhere.

"Are you okay?" I asked.

He responded with irritation, "I don't want these clothes!"

I couldn't help but groan. This was the *third* time he had complained about his outfit. Trying to be as calm as possible, I suggested a different outfit. He kept shaking his head, disapproving of all my suggestions. After I picked the fifth outfit, he once again threw himself on the floor.

Here was this kid I was making breakfast for, this kid I was helping to get ready so I could drop him off at his nursery. This child was someone I was sacrificing almost all of my time for, and yet he was acting like this!

The thoughts kept forming in my mind. Immediately, I felt an angry heat rising in my chest. My hands started shaking, my face turned red, and my heart pounded away. I threw the clothes on the floor. Lashing out, I yelled,

What did you just say? I'm going to spank the hell out of you if you don't put these clothes on right now!

My son still didn't listen. I had to angrily force him into the outfit, ignoring his tears when he started crying.

Still fuming, I dropped him off at school. Later, as I got settled in at work, I regretted my actions. I must confess, that morning wasn't my finest moment.

I'm usually not an angry person. However, since I became a mother, I'd been experiencing more moments of rage than I cared to admit.

If only I had known half of what I know now, things would've been different. Luckily for you, you are already on your life-changing journey.

Let's start by recognizing that anger is a natural human emotion. While anger may be a good thing sometimes, i.e., when it gives you the energy to get something done, it can also have negative effects. Below, we'll take a look at *why* you get angry and why you feel even angrier than others.

The Damaging Lies about Parenting

Becoming a parent can change your life drastically. As you watch your child grow, you may begin to wonder what it even means to be a parent. In its most basic definition, being a parent means you are either the mother or father of a child.

However, the act of parenting is much more than that.

What then is parenting? What does it mean to you?

Recognizing what parenting means to you helps you create a meaningful definition of the concept for yourself. This definition will support and guide you on the roller coaster that is parenthood.

Let's face it. Parenting can be confusing, complicated, broad, diverse, confrontational, difficult, and tiring. Some of us are better equipped to take on this demanding job, but others find it difficult to cope. Most parents fall back on what they know intuitively. They also rely on advice from others. All of this information combines to form their core beliefs about parenting.

Your beliefs determine how you act, and harboring wrong beliefs can lead to wrongdoings. For example, some good people may turn out to be bad at parenting because of some unhealthy beliefs they were taught. Therefore, it's important to **know that not all parenting beliefs or pieces of advice are helpful.**

The following are some common myths you should avoid:

Myth 1: Parenting is about fixing your child.

I once held a certain misconception about parenting. I thought parenting was about prompting kids to act in certain ways. Specifically, *my* ways. I believed that once I "fixed" my child by changing his behavior, everything else would become easy.

That thinking was so wrong!

Of course, we want our kids to be in control of their emotions for good reason. No parent wants to deal with their kid being fussy or throwing a tantrum anytime they don't have their way.

Suppose you keep telling your child to clean up after playing with their toys, but they never listen. In this case, you'll likely think you must *fix* their attitude so they don't become unorganized and irresponsible adults.

Another example is when you keep ensuring that your child uses their right hand to eat and write. You might do this because you know some cultures view using the left hand to do these things as wrong. At this point, you might feel the need to fix your child, thinking doing so is for their own good.

Over the years, I've realized that parenting is largely about the *parent* (you) and not just the child.

Myth 2: Parenting is about raising "good" kids.

What's your definition of "good?"

Do you consider your child to be "good" if they're obedient, pay attention, have self-control, and earn high grades? You might also assume a "good" kid allows you to sleep throughout the night without worrying. They don't throw tantrums when they don't get what they want, and you don't receive calls from the school because they didn't get into trouble. So-called "good kids" get high grades in school, and they don't involve themselves in social vices such as drugs. Generally, parenting these kids is viewed as easy.

There's a problem with this thinking, however. When our kids don't meet those specific expectations of a "good" kid, we then tend to label their other actions as "bad."

Rather than worrying about applying labels to our kids, we should instead focus on analyzing why we get bothered and angered by their behavior.

Myth 3: Parenting is about making our children excel.

Parenting is not about forcing our kids to get good grades or be the best performer in a group. Instead, we should strive to always support our kids and help them achieve their potential. But often, we seem to forget what the word "potential" even means.

When considering their potential, are we trying to coax them into reaching something they don't even have yet? For example, are we trying to have them study math before the semester begins only for the sole purpose of getting better grades?

I've come to realize that parenting isn't about ensuring my child gets that high score or performs the best out of his peer group. Doing so means we often forget the amazing qualities they already possess by constantly looking at what the future *could* hold.

Myth 4: Parenting is all about raising a happy child.

What is your number one wish for your child? I'm guessing it relates to their happiness. Of course, many parents want their kids to be happy for most of their lives. There's no issue with wanting this. However, it does become an issue when we assume that happiness is something our kid needs to find before acquiring it.

As parents, it can be hard to watch when your child feels sad or disappointed over something you can't control. You want to make them happy quickly by providing short-term relief. Sometimes this short-term relief is extra screen time watching their favorite cartoon. Other times, you might buy them an expensive gift or even allow them to play video games they wouldn't normally be allowed to play.

I've learned that parenting isn't just about making our kids happy. It's far from it! We shouldn't always shield them from the disappointments in life. Rather, we should teach them how they can successfully ride the waves of disappointment.

Unfortunately, life is full of these misfortunes, and it's not helpful to suggest we can always avoid them.

Myth 5: Parenting is all about controlling your kid.

Do you consider your good parenting days to be the days you can "make" your kids get along? Maybe you think a good parenting day is when they don't question your routine and listen to everything you tell them.

In your eyes, bad parenting might be the complete opposite. You might think you're a bad parent if your kid challenges you and diminishes your sense of control. On those days when they test your patience, whine, or throw tantrums, you likely become angry with their behaviors. Why?

Because you aren't in control.

But why do you care so much about being in control? Where does this need for total control stem from? Why do you want it so badly?

Many parents feel they need to be in control to guide kids in the right direction. They don't want their kids to make bad choices or go against the values they've worked to instill in them.

We also see our kids as a product of parenting. For example, if we're used to eating certain foods, our kids should also follow suit. We want to mold them in the way we envision, forgetting that we *can't* always control them.

Remember, we don't want to be control freaks.

Why Are You Angrier Than Other Parents?

If you stop and reflect for a while, you'll notice that you're probably treating your child the same way your parents treated you as a child. For example, my mom used to tell me, " You got that from your dad" whenever I had a low grade at school or when I did something wrong at home.

This phrase was something I didn't like to hear. In fact, I hated hearing that statement over and over. However, it was shocking to realize that I was saying the exact thing to my son when he did something similar. *"OMG! Am I slowly becoming my mom?"* I asked myself. The thought was terrifying!

The roots of our tendency to lash out can be traced to our early years. Many of us enter the world of parenting with our own childhood wounds that haven't healed. It's important to recognize how deeply our childhood experiences influenced us. It's equally crucial to understand why we all respond differently and how those responses affect our parenting approach today.

A Burmese proverb reads, *"Parents are the first teachers of children."* This line of thought is true. The things your parents did, the things they said to you, and how they related and reacted to you all lay the foundation for your behaviors, beliefs, attitude, and parenting style.

These characteristics were transmitted mostly through your everyday interactions with your parents. Subconsciously, you tuned into the messages they sent. This absorption of their messages influenced how you view yourself and the world around you.

Sometimes, parents may intentionally recreate experiences from their childhood with their own child. For example, you may enjoy taking your child for a bike ride in the park because you did this with your parents when you were younger.

On the other hand, some parents intentionally try to do the opposite of what their parents did. For example, a dad may decide never to make his kid eat certain foods because his own parents forced him to eat that food against his will. Similarly, a mom may decide to show affection to her child and could even become overly emotional because she never got any affection from her parents.

Many times, you might let your anger take over as you go down memory lane. Your reaction to a situation with your child might stem from your own childhood experiences, beliefs, and values. There's a good chance you're not even yet aware of when this is happening.

Fortunately, there's a way you can become more aware of these reactions. First, you'll need to consider your own childhood experiences.

Ask yourself the following questions:

- How have your parents impacted you? Positively or negatively?
- How was anger expressed in your family while you were growing up?
- How did your father/mother express anger?

- What was happening during your childhood when you were the age your child is now?
- Are you acting or sounding just like your parents in a way you aren't proud of?
- Are you projecting your childhood experiences onto your child?
- Have your parents raised you in ways you don't want to recreate with your child?

As you reflect on these questions, you'll likely stir up strong feelings. Consider discussing these emotions with your partner, a trusted friend, or even a professional. Reflecting on your childhood can help you unpack your past and become a better parent.

CHAPTER 2

UNDERSTANDING PARENTING TRIGGERS

*"Never do anything when you have a temper,
for you will do everything wrong."*

— Baltasar Gracian

"Oh no! I swore I wasn't going to yell at my son anymore. Why have I failed to keep to my word yet again?"*

As a parent, you definitely know when an emotional storm is on the horizon. You feel it in your body. Your blood starts boiling, and you become helpless to stop the rage that follows. When the storm finally hits, that's when you lose control. You start screaming at the top of your lungs, trying to control your kids.

I had just finished cleaning the kitchen and was rushing to bathe my child before bedtime. When I walked into his room, I saw him playing games on his iPad. I asked him to stop, but he ignored me. I resorted to forcefully pulling the device out of his hand. Unfortunately, the iPad fell, its screen breaking in the process.

Immediately, I felt the storm coming. I was full of rage and felt like I was about to explode. And then I knew what happened. I had been triggered.

Do We All Have Triggers?

Of course, we all have triggers, regardless of whether they're big or small. Triggers are elements of an experience that cause emotional reactions. Have you ever felt your chest tighten upon hearing your child make a seemingly minor comment? The comment may not seem like a big deal to others, but it is to you. This "not-such-a-big-deal" comment shuts you down for the rest of the day, filling you with rage, anxiety, or shame. That comment was a trigger.

But why do we all have triggers?

The answer is quite simple! Triggers are a result of unresolved feelings. Perhaps during your childhood, you found it hard to cope with certain intense feelings. The more helpless you felt as a child, the more vulnerable you were to trauma.

Some examples of situations that often reveal unresolved trauma include:

- Being blamed or shamed
- Being controlled
- Being ignored or discounted by someone
- Rejection from someone you care about
- Seeing a disapproving look on your child
- Feeling helpless in difficult situations
- Your child judging you
- Isolation from someone you love

These examples should get you thinking about possible circumstances that could cause you to react intensely.

Clues That Show You Are Being Triggered

Most times, we aren't aware of our triggers until after an irrational, over-the-top reaction. We then start noticing that *something* triggered us. Some parents report not believing that the past is truly the past. They say this because when they're triggered, they feel shoved back into the past as if they're reliving the original experience.

While my son was growing up, my husband always said I was overreacting to my son's behavior. My anger boils when my son talks back to me, yet my husband doesn't mind when our son does the same to him. I yell when my son wants to sleep without changing into his pajamas, but it doesn't bother my husband.

He always says, *"It's okay. It's not a big deal."*

We're parents of the same child, but we have different reactions to his behavior. In the past, I always wondered why. My husband and I were from different family backgrounds and the way he was raised was very different from my own experience. His very calm childhood means he rarely gets angry now, unlike me. I grew up in a family that cared about little things and was quick to give consequences to actions.

The following are ways to spot triggers when they manifest:

- When your child makes you feel very sad, and you recall having the same experience in the past, this may signal a trigger.
- When your child does or says something that makes you angry to the extent of yelling, that action could be a trigger.
- When you're furious and feel like spanking your child, you could be experiencing a trigger.

Why should you recognize your triggers?

Unresolved trauma in the past can pass through generations, continuing to affect a family for a long period if left unresolved. Knowing your triggers can help you increase your chances of showing a positive response to your child's emotions.

If you've identified your triggers that lead to irrational and damaging responses, you can then take steps to resolve the situation. It is only once you recognize your triggers that you can respond proactively and positively.

7 Most Common Parenting Triggers

If you keep losing your cool more than you'd like, here are common triggers that may be behind your actions.

1. Crying

A child's constant cry can send parents into panic mode. The tears can elicit strong emotions in you that make you feel anxious, afraid, confused, resentful, and angry. Many parents weren't lovingly supported or listened to when they were kids. As parents, we see the crying itself as the problem. In truth, it's often the only way for a child to communicate their needs. On the downside, it can trigger uncomfortable feelings for us.

2. Whining

Whining is a common trigger for parents as well. It often gets on your nerves, especially when your kid won't stop doing it. If a child won't take NO for an answer and keeps repeating the unwanted behavior, it can trigger certain emotions in you. For example, your child may want to have more snacks even when you've given them one already. When you tell them no more snacks, they start whining to make you agree to their demands.

3. Disrespect

Some of us were disrespected as kids, and getting disrespected by our own kids can be very triggering.

Has your child ever talked back to you or mimicked your words when you're scolding them? Perhaps when you ask them to read a book or do their homework instead of watching TV, they roll their eyes. Maybe they scoff and say, *"Whatever!"*

You might feel disrespected when you talk to them, and they pretend they didn't hear you. Other signs of disrespect can be as extreme as disregarding your rules by coming home late even when you asked them not to, saying hurtful things like calling you a bad mom, or even showing physical aggression.

4. Saying "I hate you"

Hearing the phrase "I hate you" coming from anyone can be very hurtful, especially when it's coming from your own child. However, it's their own way of communicating that they are mad, confused, angry, or upset. They don't know how else to communicate the extent of their feelings, and they resorted to this phrase.

These words can be very painful for parents to hear from a child they love so much, triggering some intense emotions.

5. Being physically hurt

A trigger can be as extreme as your child physically hurting you. Your child may be physical with you by accident or because they want to get your attention. As a result, you lose it. They may pull your hair, kick the back of your seat in the car, or tug on your clothes. For example, my son once headbutted me, and I bled in the process of trying to bathe him. Immediately, I felt a flash response and started shouting at him.

6. Siblings fighting

Fights between siblings can be a big trigger, too. This situation wasn't a problem for me because I have just one child. However, I've watched other people get triggered because their kids are fighting.

When one of your kids is rude or aggressive to the other, the action may tip off a response in you. Often, you can't help but lash out. This reaction can even be traced to your childhood experiences where your sibling got away with many things because they were older, and you don't want your kids to relive that experience. Lashing out is your way of attempting to set limits.

7. Spills and accidents

This is another trigger that can cause problems. I mentioned earlier how I took my son's iPad from him, and the screen broke when it fell. My emotions were so overwhelming that I couldn't control them.

Spills and accidents can drive many parents crazy, especially when they're already on edge. We don't treat these episodes as an accident. Instead, we react immediately, even if we feel remorseful later.

Choosing Your Battles

Correcting kids for their wrongdoings each time can wear any parent out quickly. They're just kids trying to learn how the world works, and they're bound to make errors during this learning phase.

Choosing your battles means being selective of the arguments, problems, and confrontations that you get into with your child. Instead of fighting all of these issues, let the kid win sometimes but "fight to win" when it's time to set boundaries. Not knowing the battles to choose can overwhelm you and increase your anger.

You can choose your battles by:

1. Letting them win

You may need to lose the smaller battles to win the war ahead. Recognize the small battles that you can let slide. If you keep fighting all the time, your child will eventually view your behavior as nagging.

Allowing them to win is also a way of establishing independence. For instance, it's natural for parents to feel concerned about their child's nutrition. Instead of always forcing certain fruits and veggies on them because you fear they'll become malnourished, why not give them multiple options and let them choose what they like?

I didn't eat many veggies growing up (especially carrots and spinach. Yuck!), but I turned out fine.

While some kids prefer to relax a little before doing their homework, others like doing it immediately after school. Allow your kid to decide how and when they want to do their homework, especially when it leads to positive results.

2. Fighting to win

Here, there is no room for mistakes. There are times when you need to enforce rules and make sure your child abides by them. In these instances, it's for their own good. They need to understand why you stepped in to handle things the "adult way."

There are some basic things they should know and heed to. For example, they need to know that brushing their teeth twice daily will prevent cavities, and going to bed early is also important because the right amount of sleep is needed for good health.

Fighting to win can also involve creating a no-phone zone. For example, the bathroom, dinner table, school, and other places that don't require a phone can be a no-phone zone. When in these areas, they should respect this rule and keep their phones away.

Assigning chores to kids is also important. If they have chores that aren't complete, you'll need to win this battle. Whether it's making their beds, unloading the dishwasher, or watering the flower beds, you need to prioritize these chores. Your child will eventually enjoy the reward, even if that time doesn't come until adulthood.

Finally, when you encounter difficulty establishing the rules, remember the words of Margaret Thatcher: *"You may have to fight a battle more than once to win it."*

In the next chapter, we'll dig deeper by examining the power struggle between parents and their kids. We'll discuss how this tussle can be the cause of your anger and how you can eliminate it.

CHAPTER 3

WHY DO YOU GET ANGRY AT YOUR CHILDREN?

*"The kids who need the most love will ask for
it in the most unloving of ways"*

— Unknown

You aren't alone if you've asked yourself why you are always getting angry with your child. Many moms revealed being frustrated from yelling, screaming, and trying to be in control of their kids.

Both children and parents have a need for control. A toddler might insist on wanting more ice cream instead of a healthier snack, or your teenager doesn't want to go out for dinner after you yell at them repeatedly. But, unfortunately, your screams fell on deaf ears, and you ultimately felt disrespected.

We all want to raise our kids to be fair, understanding, kind, and patient. We know what's best for them, and we want them to listen to us and heed our advice. But when we don't get the reaction we want from them, we find ourselves in a power struggle, Parents vs. Kids.

This chapter explains how these power struggles play out and how you can minimize them. By the end of the chapter, you should be able to identify the reasons why you easily enter fight mode with your kids.

Understanding Power Struggles

Power struggles are essentially fights. A typical parent-child power struggle is when your child refuses to do something and you continue to insist. You keep telling them, *"Do it now!" or "If you don't do this, there will be consequences!"* or *"You're going to regret not doing this!"*

The continuous disagreements between kids and parents can become a battle of wills. For example, when you say "Yes," your child will say "No." As the argument continues, it becomes even more difficult to get the child to comply. As a parent, we feel we must end the struggle to regain power. Yet this is exactly the reason behind your anger!

In these types of battles, we often feel that our child challenges our power. As a result, we then exert more power to ensure our child complies. Unfortunately, the more we try to demonstrate this power, the more likely it is for our kids to throw tantrums or keep telling us "no."

This seemingly endless cycle can be very frustrating, pushing us to that boiling point. But unfortunately, at this stage, we often forget why we are establishing a limit in the first place. Instead, we become absorbed with the idea of who is in charge.

Many parents find themselves in this exact situation. Power struggles are part of every family's life. As parents, you're faced with the continuous problem of getting your child to do a certain thing and making sure they do that thing at a specific time.

To work through this part of life, you'll need to combine both your expectations as a parent and your child's wants. These desires may collide sometimes. When that happens, it'll likely feel like a lose-lose situation for both you and your child. You may feel misunderstood, disrespected, powerless, or even resentful afterward. Your child likely ends up feeling the same way.

I want you to take a minute to evaluate the relationship you have with your child. How often do you experience power struggles? If these struggles come up, are they major or minor? Do a lot of emotions flare up at these times? How do you and your child feel about each other after an argument?

When we enter a power struggle with our children, we usually recall past parenting mantras passed onto us. These instilled beliefs might be: "Never allow a child to have the upper hand!" or "Don't give in. That'll make them think you're weak," or "If you give them an inch, they'll take a mile."

When these sentiments echo in our minds, we also feel shame and disapproval. We might feel like undisciplined parents who allow our children to make silly mistakes. These ultra-strict viewpoints are slowly becoming obsolete. While our parents and grandparents made an effort to prove they were their children's absolute bosses, today's parenting culture is different.

There is less black-and-white thinking in this new style of parenting. Parents actively seek ways to reduce power struggles between themselves and their kids. This method helps the family enjoy a more fulfilling and intimate relationship. Today, parenting is more about **collaboration and mutual understanding** between parents and their kids.

As we learned from choosing your battles in the previous chapter, giving your kids choices doesn't mean you are losing your power as a parent. In fact, you still have full control of the situation.

Remember, becoming a peaceful parent means you're learning to help your kids make better choices, not getting into fights with them. Your child shouldn't be viewed as an opponent but as a human that needs love.

Start giving choices like these instead:

Don't say: "If you don't brush your teeth now, there'll be no screen time for you tomorrow." "If you don't clean up your room now, there won't be a playdate for you next week." " Wear these black pants for tomorrow, period."

Try this instead: "If you don't brush your teeth, I'll help brush them for you." "If you clean your room quickly, we can play together." "Choose either your black or your gray pants for school tomorrow."

7 Signs That You Are an Angry Parent

We all experience anger at varying levels. Sometimes, expressing this anger can be healthier than keeping it all hidden inside. However, while it's okay to express your anger in a productive manner, letting out uncontrollable anger shows your ugly side.

Parental anger is definitely not the most comfortable emotion to experience. It's even worse when you have to deal with the consequences that follow afterward. If you find yourself getting angry more than usual, it might be a sign of a serious problem.

Therefore, the signs below indicate when anger has become a problem.

1. You Get Angry Frequently

How many times do you explode when driving home with your kids? Do you get angry at even the slightest inconvenience? For example, you might get angry because your kids come to the dinner table late. Do you get overly upset when you have to clean up after them or when there's a minor problem like they're walking to the car too slowly?

Think about your reaction. Are your outbursts reasonable?

If you notice that you frequently lose control or get angry constantly at your child, don't overlook this problem.

2. Your Kids Are Scared of You

Do you hurt your kids physically or verbally? Does your child avoid making eye contact with you?

Do you think violent behavior like slamming doors, punching walls, shouting, snapping, yelling, or calling your kids' names are normal responses? Of course, you can raise your voice sometimes to get a kid's attention but never to the point where they get scared of you.

If you sense fear in them, it means you've gone too far. How do you want your kid to remember you? As a scary mom? That's not what any parent wants.

3. You Have A Short Temper

Do you yell at your kids at the slightest provocation? Do you need to always scream out your child's name to summon them? Do you suddenly burst into anger at a moment's notice?

If you have a short fuse, you probably constantly yell. Trivial things make you furious. For example, you might get angry because your child forgot to bring their lunch bag to school. Maybe you explode because your kids dropped their toys in the hallway or put their shoes on the wrong feet. The inability to control your temper around your kids is a clear sign of parental anger issues.

4. You Have No Patience

Have you tried to be patient with your kids?

Suppose you get very anxious when your kids aren't ready when it's time to go somewhere, or you start yelling right after you discover your kid hasn't done their homework.

Maybe you yell, "Hurry up!" but they drag their feet, even though they need to catch the bus. Maybe you get stressed when they take forever to get ready for school. If these minor situations cause you to lose it and start cursing, you probably have limited patience.

5. Always Blaming Others

Do you always find a way to blame your kids, saying their actions are what's making you angry? For example, imagine you mistakenly drop your favorite sunglasses on the couch and your child unknowingly sits on them and breaks them. Do you blame your child for not looking and say it is their fault?

Another example could be that your child tells you he wants to go to the bathroom right before leaving the house in the morning. You end up being late for both school and work. Do you blame your child for making you get to work late and keep reminding them of it?

6. Your Kids Say You're Angry

This one resonates with me, as much as I don't want to admit it. My son, one of the dearest people to me, once walked up to me and asked why I was always angry. I knew right there that my anger had become a problem, and I needed to fix things.

If you recently heard from your kids, spouse, friends, or someone else that you're often angry, it's time to think about where you are right now.

"Are you mad at me, Mom?"

"Mommy, why do you always yell at me?" "Did I make you mad again, Mom?"

If these sorts of questions sound familiar, think about how often you show your frustration and irritation to your child. Your child shouldn't see you as an angry parent. They need to know you as the loving parent that cares for them.

7. You're Not Open to Accepting and Forgiving

How do you feel when your kid says something bad about you? Do you get mad? How long does it take for you to forgive them? People that aren't open to accepting and forgiving take a long time to get over problems. Your kids may say something that triggers feelings of rage in you, and it takes longer than normal to move past the issue.

Maybe your child says something like *"You're so mean, Mom!"* or *"I wish you weren't my mom."* This makes it difficult to control your anger, and you can't seem to accept and forgive them. Kids' words can sadden their parents, and some have an especially hard time coping with it. The parents start thinking about how they've sacrificed so much for their child, only to hear them say such hurtful words.

■ ■ ■

Which of the above signs can you relate to? Do you think you're an angry parent? If you think you are, it's okay because this book will provide you with all the help you need. Thankfully, you already have awareness, which is a great place to start.

Reflective questions

To manage your anger as a parent, you need to learn more about your anger's causes and triggers. To start, answer the following questions:

- **Why/When** does your anger occur?
- **Why** do you always yell?
- **What** memories trigger a reaction from you?
- **What** are people's reactions when you become angry?

As you answer these questions, you'll become more aware of the reasons for your anger as well as the problems that result from it.

The next chapter discusses your child's anger and how you can help them deal with it effectively.

PART 2

WHO OWNS THE PROBLEM, YOU OR YOUR CHILD?

CHAPTER 4

UNDERSTANDING CHILDREN'S ANGER

*"The child needs a helping hand or he'll grow up
to be an angry young man someday."*

— Elvis Presley

How do you react when your child is rude to you, hits their sibling, refuses to do their homework, or says, *"I hate you!"*?

What do you think causes the anger that makes them scream in the shopping mall or break things on the floor?

To answer these questions, let's start with the basics. Adults and kids aren't so different. They both want to always feel good and be loved. When these needs aren't met, we struggle with expressing ourselves. If a child gets angry, it's usually because they don't know how to ask for what they need. They also may not have learned how to take "no" as an answer.

As my son was growing up, it was clear he was smart and strong-minded. However, he expressed these traits by throwing or hitting objects, saying horrible things, and screaming at the top of his lungs. This always made me feel like I was a terrible mom. However, I later came to understand his behaviors and the anger that caused them.

In this chapter, I share the knowledge I've learned and discuss ways and why children misbehave. Knowing the cause of your kid's anger can help you deal with it more effectively.

Why Do Children Misbehave?

Do you know why your kids misbehave? Do you think they misbehave because they *want* to see you angry?

I believe that when you were a child, misbehaving meant something different to you then than it does now. What misbehavior signifies depends on exactly what it was your child does and how you perceive the behavior. Sometimes, children's misbehavior can be intentional, and other times, it isn't. A child's age is a big factor that has nothing to do with intention. For example, a toddler is bound to "misbehave" since they don't know what is right or what's wrong at this early stage.

When your child does something against your wishes, it's easy to react with resentment, frustration, and anger. For example, think about a time when you might be running late for work, shopping in the grocery store, on your way to dinner, or trying to catch a bus last minute. These situations might already put you on edge.

When your child misbehaves, you might react in an awful way. Maybe you even say things like, *"What the hell is wrong with you!"* or *"Are you dumb?"* or *"I wish you'd never been born."*

Parents with kids that misbehave usually wonder how they can deal with their children's actions. As your child grows, they're inevitably exposed to new conditions and environments. Discomfort in these uncertain situations can cause them to act out.

You'll find the following section helpful if you and your child have been on this road yourselves.

7 Reasons Why Children Misbehave

First, ask yourself:

"Why is my child acting this way?" "What do they gain when they misbehave?"

Our kids misbehave for many reasons. Once we identify these reasons, we can better understand how to solve the problem.

The following are seven common reasons children misbehave.

1. When they don't feel well

Every child needs to eat well, get fresh air, exercise, and, most importantly, sleep well. Without meeting these basic needs, your child won't feel their best. They'll become hard to get along with and are more likely to act out.

If your child is tired, for example, they'll likely get cranky and nothing besides sleep will fix the problem. A hungry child will also become irritable and make even minor tasks tiring for you. Likewise, inactive children will become bored, which can translate into equally grouchy behavior!

Rather than focusing on the so-called "misbehaviors," remember that your children's negative actions are really alerting you to a problem that needs your attention.

2. When they feel rejected

"I can't fit in anywhere!" "My mom will never like me!"

Sound familiar?

A child who feels unwanted will likely say these sorts of things. They also tend to be moody, resentful, and even misbehave. Perhaps they feel you've ignored their feelings and thoughts for so long that they've started seeing themselves as unworthy of love.

When your child feels you've rejected them, they grow more insecure and anxious. These feelings can lead to low self-esteem, self-doubt, and depression over time. Your child may become aggressive and hostile towards you.

Note that their misbehavior may not end in childhood. The emotional pain of rejection may linger into adulthood.

3. When they feel unloved

"I'm not good enough. No one loves me!" "I can't do anything right!"

How do you feel when you hear your child say these sorts of things?

A child that doesn't feel loved will give the same unpleasant feelings back. In other words, they'll think and act in an unloving way, too. Children *like* pleasing who they love. But if they can't have a loving relationship with their mom, they don't have a reason to behave correctly other than to avoid punishment. While you may love your child, knowing in your heart you love them isn't enough. They must know it as well.

How can you show your affection? Many children understand signs of love, such as hugs, kisses, smiles, pats, kind words, etc.

4. When they lack knowledge and experience

Children are children! You don't need to assume they are mini-adults. They make mistakes through their actions just as they make mistakes when putting on their shoes or counting numbers. These errors are all normal parts of their growing-up experiences.

Children don't have the knowledge and experience adults have. You know better than them. For example, when a child hits another child, they may not know that hitting is unacceptable. They may not clean their room because they don't know what to do when their toys don't fit into their toy box.

In these cases, instead of giving your child a consequence, you can show them what to do. Teach them the alternatives to misbehaviors to help them learn from their mistakes.

5. When they are upset or insecure

It's difficult to accept and adjust to change, especially for kids. Change can upset our children and make them act in surprising ways. What do changes in a child's life look like? They might come when your entire family moves to a different neighborhood when a mother is sick when a new baby arrives or when they switch grades in school.

Your child will likely feel insecure when their regular routines are affected. As a result, they'll need regular assurance. Otherwise, their discomfort can turn into misbehaving.

6. When they lack confidence

A child needs to feel like they can follow their dreams, and it's your job to make them feel capable. A confident child wants to try new things and approach unfamiliar tasks without fear.

But when a child feels inadequate, they may compensate by bragging, boasting, or even becoming aggressive. They may begin to withdraw from others and not be open to trying out new things. A child with the idea they "can't do anything" will cover up their lack of confidence with misbehaviors.

7. When they feel discouraged

As kids grow, they need to be pointed in the right direction. They need approval, encouragement, and kind words from their parents.

Parents often forget that their kids need to be encouraged. They don't realize that when their child gets their approval, that helps them feel good and act in healthy ways. They are more likely to maintain the same good behavior to get that **good** feeling again.

On the other hand, if kids don't receive praise for the good things they do, they may start misbehaving to get your attention.

It's surprising, but I've realized our culture is more tolerant of pets misbehaving than babies. For example, many people are quick to react negatively (or even curse) when their toddler is crying or throwing a tantrum than when their dog whines and barks.

Have you ever noticed how people react when a toddler cries in a park or restaurant compared to a dog barking continuously? People won't pay much attention to the dog, but the baby is seen as disturbing the peace.

Society's judgment of babies vs. pets is an indication that part of our mindset needs to be changed. If you think a parent should punish a crying kid at the park, you've failed to recognize that one of the child's basic needs hasn't been met.

All Behavior Is Communication

Sometimes, children's misbehavior may feel personal, like they are intentionally doing it to complicate your life. We have to remember that everyday life is stressful. Your child's negative behavior only feels intentional because it's fueling your already high stress levels.

But what if you think of your child's misbehavior as a method of communication? Consider it their way of reaching out to you. As adults, parents can easily practice decoding and managing their feelings. Kids on the other hand are still learning communication skills. Instead of voicing they are bored and hungry, they may do seemingly irrational things like throwing their toys away.

Even though some children's behavior is negative and undesirable, the motive isn't. Those negative behaviors they exhibit don't make them bad kids. There's a significant difference between how your child behaves and their character.

Their actions aren't who they are.

Everyone communicates through behavior, even if it's in different ways. While an infant cries when hungry, an adult will yawn when bored or tired. Both humans are communicating something even if they aren't aware.

Children *want* to communicate their needs. They aren't crying or throwing tantrums for no reason. As parents, you need to pay close attention to your child's behavior and decipher what they're trying to communicate. Remember that kids may engage in challenging behaviors because they want to get their parent's attention. They may also do it to get out of an activity they dislike or are simply bored. But no matter the mode of communication, there is always a reason behind the behavior.

While your child is expressing their anger through negative behavior, don't try to change the behavior itself. Doing so often results in your child feeling unloved and unheard, only increasing the rage.

Trying to address the negative behavior could lead to a power struggle, which is what you want to avoid. So instead, after your child calms down, identify why they were upset. Listen carefully to what they say. This way, they won't need to throw a pillow on the floor or break a glass cup next time before they are heard.

Once they realize they are heard, many kids will want to clean the mess immediately and apologize. They know their parents watch and listen to them, and that ultimately, they are there to help them.

If your child repeatedly misbehaves, it's time to stop and examine yourself. Trust me. It's easier to prevent misbehaviors before they occur than to try to deal with them as they're happening.

Now, ask yourself:

- *Are the rules I've set for my kids **reasonable**?*

- *Am I using more **do's** than don'ts for them?*
- *Is there **consistency** with the way I enforce rules?*
- *Am I giving my kids enough **choices** to make?*
- *Am I making it **easy** for my child to behave well?*
- *Do I **play** with my kids?*

Remember, your child's brain is still growing and is in the process of being rewired. They are developing a more logical thought process that makes them want to question your opinions and ideas.

As a result, they are going to be argumentative. Of course, this tendency can make you feel frustrated and even angrier. Keep in mind that expressing love during anger can be difficult, and you may even be tempted to respond to your child with negative and condemning words. However, it's important that you don't allow your emotions to dictate your behaviors (or your child's).

The next chapter will discuss your own anger and how it can complicate an already unpleasant situation.

CHAPTER 5

DO YOU MAKE THINGS WORSE?

"Nobody can misunderstand a child as much as his own parents."

— Sydney J. Harris

Different situations make people angry. Your child may be rude to you or break down in tears when you're trying to correct them, fueling your anger. You might even get so angry you don't heed the speed limit, resulting in trouble with the police. You might get triggered by something small, but your instinct will be to scream, yell, or even just vent. These are all natural responses.

However, the fact that it's natural doesn't mean your response is a good idea. While yelling might make you feel better for a while, it doesn't solve the main problem.

Getting angry at your child for throwing a tantrum and crying will only encourage them to do it more. It sure won't stop them.

This chapter discusses how parents make an already "bad" situation worse. You'll learn how to address the issue with your kids and see that even a slight change in your actions can significantly reduce anger triggers.

Let's start with understanding how a wrong interpretation of your child's expression can worsen a situation.

You Are Bad At Interpreting

In the previous chapter, we discussed how your child's misbehavior could be a form of communication. If you can't identify what your child is trying to communicate or if you misinterpret it, problems are going to happen.

You may be wondering how misinterpretation happens between you and your own child. After all, no one knows them better than you do. How could you possibly misunderstand their message?

Think about it like this. As your anger grows, you start thinking irrationally. You may think that your child's misbehavior is even intentional. I mentioned earlier that when your child misbehaves, they aren't doing it to drive you mad. Rather, your child needs or wants something. For example, if you ask your child to clean their room and they don't, you shouldn't assume they're being disrespectful. When you think about the situation objectively, you'll likely see that they just want to play more games, have fun with their toys, or even relax. There are no bad intentions behind their refusal to clean their room, and they certainly aren't trying to make you feel bad.

Let's consider the last time you got angry and lost control.

Maybe you'd had a long day at work. Perhaps you were tired, and something your child said or did triggered you. Whatever the reason, there was a bigger reason you lost your temper than the actual trigger. Use this place as a starting point for identifying misinterpretation.

Many of us misinterpret our kids' behavior because we're expecting them to do things beyond their abilities. For instance, when a baby cries, you might get annoyed by their cries and think they're acting unusual. But that's what babies do! The infant won't understand your reactions. In short, your expectations should be appropriate for your child's age.

When children don't behave the way we want them to, we often misinterpret the behavior. We may assume they're being defiant instead of looking at the situation from the child's point of view. When a child makes a fuss, we may assume that they want to disturb our peace. In reality, the child may be hurt, hungry, or feel ill from a stomach ache. They don't know how else to express their need and will resort to crying.

You may feel annoyed and tempted to yell, but something as easy as rocking the baby to sleep can help. Yet, we as parents tend to overlook these simple possibilities. We get so focused on making sure we have control of the situation that we often assume the worst about our kids.

You've probably heard the adage "Work smarter, not harder." This saying applies to parenting, too. Sometimes, the simple solution is the one that works the best, although that can feel counterintuitive.

We expect our kids to calmly tell us what they want so we can solve their problems. But we keep forgetting that effective communication is a life skill that requires time to develop.

My Kid Listens To Me Only When I Yell

"I always try not to yell… I really am trying. However, it doesn't change anything because it seems like yelling is the only way I can get my kids to listen to me."

I've heard moms say this countless times. Eventually, I help them understand that they have it all wrong.

Do you really think your kids only listen to you when you yell at them? If so, why do you think yelling is required for your kids to do something right?

Even though many parents believe they need to yell before being heard, it's not true. How long can yelling help you? Also consider the bigger question: Is yelling what you want your kids to respond to?

It may be a little effective when your kids are younger, but it won't give you your desired result when they become older. You need to develop a more effective way of getting your kids to listen that doesn't involve yelling. Instead of adding to your home's tension by shouting, you'll need to address the root of the problem and figure out how you can stop this pattern of yelling.

Too often, parents tend to repeat themselves until they are blue in the face. Unfortunately, their kids still won't listen, so they end up yelling out of frustration.

I've been in this struggle myself in the past. My stress levels would increase, a power struggle would begin, and yelling seemed to be the only way I could get my son to listen (or so I thought).

I soon found myself on a slippery slope. My house was filled with bargaining and threats. It was exhausting to get my son to do anything without a fight. Finally, I paused and asked myself, "What exactly is going on? Why do I have to yell before my child can listen to me? How can I break this cycle and get him to listen to me?"

I was absolutely surprised when my research found that the average young child could hear up to 20 commands every 30 minutes. Imagine yourself being given a command and told to do something almost every minute of your day. You would be getting hundreds of commands a day! And we wonder why our kids don't listen to us?

Through our constant yelling, we've trained our kids to ignore us. And really, can you even blame them? Once you've heard 10 commands, you're probably going to stop listening.

Every day, parents use commands such as:

"Come here, put on your shoes, stop that, get dressed immediately, don't hit your sister, get out of bed, get in the bath, walk faster..." It's never-ending!

Put yourself in their shoes. How would you feel receiving countless commands and demands? It would definitely drive you bananas!

If you always tell your child what to do rather than offering choices, you can frustrate them. As a result, they'll tune you out. This leads to a cycle of repeating yourself and yelling before they respond.

You might assume your yelling worked, but that isn't true. The truth is, they've learned that they have many opportunities to ignore you before they listen.

They are thinking, *"It's all good; I don't have to move or answer just yet. Since she's just started getting cranky, there's plenty of time left."*

Depending on your child, they may decide to shut down and tune you out, or better still, if you have a more self-directed child, they may tell you: *"Stop telling me what to do!"* These are the kids that refuse to be bossed around.

What happens next? Your kid's behavior and disrespect drive you insane. You end up feeling overwhelmed and frustrated. So the yelling match begins.

This cycle teaches your kids to ignore you until you yell. It also teaches your kids to shout back or throw tantrums when you yell, fueling a toxic communication pattern that's detrimental to your relationship.

When you start pushing your kids to do things out of guilt, fear, and obligation, it can lead to resentment. No wonder many kids stop listening to their parents and would rather watch them yell their lungs out. This means the child has stopped caring about what their parents want. They see that the parents don't care about what they want, either.

So, how can we break this cycle? What is a more effective solution?

Engage Kids In Problem-Solving

Your child is playing games at high volume, but you're in an important Zoom meeting. You warned them to stay quiet, but they didn't listen. Your anger builds and finally explodes. You then start yelling and threatening them.

Does this situation sound familiar?

If you constantly engage in power struggles over the same issues with your child, it's time to problem-solve together. Instead, find a mutually-agreed-upon solution that can end the constant battle for power.

When a problem arises, it's natural for a parent to quickly swing into action. They want to perform the motherly or fatherly role of fixing everything. However, you may want to pipe down a bit in this situation. Please don't rush to solve your child's problem for them. Help them work through it instead.

Kids appreciate it when they know what to expect. But most times, they don't really think much about what will happen. We must tell them exactly what the problem is and what we expect from them. It's the same as giving directions to a stranger. You point to show them the place, reinforcing your words to make sure they understand. The clearer your kids are on the issue, the more likely they are to listen.

So the next time your child forgets to pack their soccer cleats or swimming bag for practice, ask them what they can do to ensure it doesn't happen again. They should develop the solutions on their own.

They might say:

- "I'll always pack my bag the night before so I don't leave anything behind."
- "I'll write a sticky note and place it on my door so I remember to pack before leaving my room."
- "I'll create a checklist to remind me of what should be in my bag." Praise your child when they provide effective solutions like these.

How You Hurt Your Child

To raise a well-rounded child, you need to form a solid support system so that they can grow up happy and with a healthy ego. However, some of us fail to realize how certain behaviors impact our children. Some of the things we do when we're angry only hurt our precious little ones and make them more likely to misbehave.

But what could a parent do to affect their kid that much?

Actions like name-calling, blaming, guilt-tripping, and shaming only cause more relationship damage.

Words we don't pay much attention to can cause severe emotional injury to our kids.

For example, it can be devastating to hear things like, *"Why can't you be like your brother?"* or *"You're a dummy!"* or *"You're so clumsy"* or *"Stop being a jerk!"* These negative labels can harm your child's personality and reduce self-esteem. They may even internalize these terms, which isn't what we want for our kids.

You may also reject your child with your words by saying, *"I wish I never had you"* or *"I wish you weren't born."* This shows that you don't love your child and want to be away from them. A child will likely feel unlovable when they feel their parent doesn't love them.

Blaming your child when they haven't done anything wrong teaches them to not take responsibility for their actions. You unfairly shift the blame to your child if you say things like:

- *"It's your fault I lost my temper."*
- *"Your sister didn't do that, you did."*
- *"I can't spend time with your father because of you."*

Kids are the easier target to blame for your actions, and unfortunately, some parents put their own feelings above their kids'.

Comparing your child with others is also something that will hurt your child. It can sow the seed of resentment in your child's mind. They may become bitter towards the person they're compared with. For example, refrain from saying things like, *"Why can't you be like our neighbor's son?"* or *"I was an "A" student when I was your age."*

Your kids are learning at their own pace. They aren't in a competition with anyone.

Another way you may be hurting your child is by shaming them. For example, you may have said something like, *"I'm so ashamed of you for acting that way today."* Words like these can make your child feel flawed and inadequate about their errors. By shaming your child, you demoralize them and do not empower change.

Cursing is one thing I used to be significantly guilty of. Later, I realized how devastating it is for a child to be verbally attacked by a parent. Words like *"Damn you!"* or *"Go to hell!"* are hostile. Kids can perceive this hostility and end up believing the worst about themselves.

Threatening your child is another way you could hurt your child without knowing. For example, saying things like, *"If you do that again, I will spank you"* or *"If you don't behave yourself, there will be no snack/screen time/playdate"* can intimidate your child. It may form fear in them to the point that they start feeling unsafe around you. Threats can be traumatizing to kids since they are vulnerable and depend on you for their basic needs.

Remember, you should never consider hitting your child, guilt-tripping, or using negative words around them. Children are not punching bags, and neither are they objects without emotions. Choose healthy ways to connect with your children.

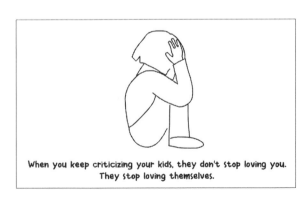

When you keep criticizing your kids, they don't stop loving you.
They stop loving themselves.

CHAPTER 6

EFFECT OF ANGRY PARENTS ON CHILDREN

"The attitude that you have as a parent is what your kids will learn from, more than what you tell them. They don't remember what you try to teach them. They remember what you are."

— Jim Henson

So far, we've discussed different aspects of anger. In this chapter, we'll focus on the effects our anger has on our kids.

While some of us think that the impact of anger is minimal as long as no one is hurt, research has suggested that parental anger has more impact on your kids than we are aware of.

Living in an environment where there is constant yelling and anger can affect a child. They get used to this form of communication and start to emulate what they've seen. Over time, this will affect their developing brain and put them at risk of mental illness later.

How Your Child Picks Up Your Anger

Have you ever wondered how your child got to the point of being so angry and aggressive? You look at your child's face and all you can see is rage. Who is to blame for this? You might think about those fictional movie characters where kids are so mean to their parents, and they end up in toxic relationships. You are hoping your situation won't turn out that way.

The truth is, your child is a product of YOU! They are still growing and don't have a hold on their emotions yet. They emulate most of the things you do, and like a boomerang, they give back what you dish out to them.

While babies vary in their level of sensitivity, they can sense and react to your emotional cues. In other words, they pick up on the emotions you give off. Because their development starts early, they rely on your emotional responses to help them interpret and react to the world around them. For example, research has shown us that babies as young as one month old can sense when their parents are angry or depressed.

Naturally, humans respond emotionally when someone else's strong emotions are displayed to them. With kids, it's even easier because their brains aren't fully developed to give a rational response yet. When they're around negative emotions, it's easy for them to notice and start repeating them.

While some kids' actions are driven by genetics, others are mainly driven by nurturing. They learn all they know about the world from you. Their adult life is shaped by their early years, making it essential for you to model good values for them.

But when they start displaying aggressive actions, it's only right for you to be worried. Some people get to a point where they begin to see themselves as a failed parent that has nurtured an angry child.

I can't even lie. I've been in your shoes, worried sick of how I got to my low point. I was so sad that life had turned out that way despite my effort. My son once pushed his food to the floor because I told him he was grounded for cursing at his friend.

Another time, he lay on the floor and cried out loud because he didn't want to do his chores. He wouldn't listen to me or take any of them to heart, which made me even angrier.

I felt so scared and needed to ask myself, *"Why is my child getting worse? Who taught him to act like this? Did he learn this in school? Do I need to change his school? Are his friends influencing him?"*

I knew children could sometimes be naughty, but my son's actions were beyond the point of naughtiness. They called for swift intervention. Finally, I came to understand that my son picked up his anger from me.

Yes, me!

I was shocked to learn this. I couldn't remember teaching my child to be in a screaming match with me, and neither did I encourage him to act wild and throw tantrums.

I stumbled upon research conducted by psychologist Albert Bandura. I learned from the research that kids could pick up social behaviors like anger by watching their *parents'* behavior. This finding opened my eyes to my own parent-son relationship. When I researched further, I had to accept that I was the catalyst for his actions.

Children, especially younger ones, see us as their role models. They tend to imitate our behaviors. Whenever we express negative emotions, our kids act out the behaviors without realizing what they're doing.

When we're stressed and dealing with a strong emotion like anger, we need to be very careful with what we say and how we act. Our kids are watching us closely, ready to emulate what we dish out.

Children don't have much control over their emotions at a very young age and are still learning emotional regulation. When a parent starts showing instability, they react similarly by throwing temper tantrums, crying more frequently, and showing excessive fear and anger.

If you look closely, you'll find your child has been in an extreme situation where you or your partner has had frequent mood swings, yelled, or name-called in front of your kids.

If what I've just described is the reality for your child, they'll get used to it. They'll think this behavior is normal. But unfortunately, they'll believe it is okay to treat other people the same way, continuing the toxic cycle. Even if you don't notice immediately, your actions can be psychologically and emotionally traumatizing for children, putting them at risk of becoming emotionally unstable.

Ultimately, a child's behaviors greatly depend on their nature, environment, what they see, and how they interpret it. Kids are like sponges, soaking up everything they know about the world from us.

When we express anger directly at our kids, they won't want to learn the values we wish to instill in them. Instead, they'll consume the emotions you present, even if they respond with silence. As parents, we must help our children know how they can do better. This lesson should be taught calmly—without yelling.

We need to start taking responsibility for our behaviors even though it's impossible to always be in a good mood. We aren't perfect and can't totally avoid getting angry. Yes, that's true! It's normal to be in a bad mood sometimes. We're going to be angry with our kids once in a while. However, it shouldn't be frequent and it should never be violent.

Parents must be in tune with their own emotions. As a parent, you must recognize when you start feeling anxious, stressed, or angry. Then, find out *why* you feel that way. Knowing the reasons will help you address them and prevent triggers from setting you off. Unfortunately, you're the only one who has control over your behavior and mood. The work is left for you to do. In Chapter 3 of this book, you learned to recognize your mood triggers, regulate your emotions, and avoid projecting how you feel on your kids. Reference the chapter again if necessary.

What Happens When You're An Angry Parent?

Have you ever wondered what influences your child's brain development? How do you want your kids to turn out? How much of a good parent do you think you are on a scale of 0 to 10?

If you can take a second to think about the effect you have on your child physically and mentally, you may be terrified of discovering the horrifying effects your anger has on your kids.

Suppose the expression of negative emotions happens frequently. In that case, it may start affecting your kid's cognitive and emotional development, which is something we should avoid at all costs.

What exactly happens to your kids when you're an angry parent?

1. It Can Cause Damage to Your Child's Emotional Development

If you're bad at managing your emotions and show aggressiveness, your child will likely mimic you and do the same. Aggressive emotions are easier to learn than positive emotions since they feel more intense and powerful.

How do you feel when someone tells you they hate you, don't want to see you, or that you disgust them?

Using hurtful words such as *"You always give me a headache!"* or *"You make my life so miserable!"* around your kids can leave a big scar mentally. These words can affect their personality, interfere with their emotional development, and make them feel worthless.

We all want what's best for our kids. Sometimes, it can be really frustrating trying to discipline them, especially when they misbehave. However, how we express our frustration can have a lasting effect on our child's development.

If done frequently, it can affect our kid's emotional development. They start being rude, aggressive, withdrawing from others, having difficulty sleeping, experiencing depression, anxiety, low self-esteem, and other emotional issues. If nothing is done, it can cause even deeper psychological problems that are carried into adulthood.

2. It Can Damage Your Child's Intellectual Development

Unfortunately, anger is an emotion that spreads like wildfire. It spreads from parents to kids quickly and soon becomes a lifestyle if nothing is done to manage it.

When your kids get anxious because of your aggression, their attention may wander.

As a result, they may not have the psychological energy to focus. They'll become stressed to the point that it starts impairing their learning. Overall, this can create an obstacle to their intellectual development.

Children who have this kind of experience usually become unstable when faced with responsibilities. In addition, seeing their parents in a bad mood again and again will create even more tension for the kids.

Depending on your child's age, they may internalize the anger received from their parents differently. While toddlers may react to negative emotions by showing anger through their actions (crying and tantrums), older kids will react emotionally. Over time, you will notice that your child won't want to relate with you and avoids you.

They may stop sharing their problems with you. These are direct effects of the negative emotions they've learned from us.

This cycle can contribute to school problems which add to your kid's doubts, guilt, and anguish. When they have poor grades in school, they tend to lose their passion to study. They may hate going to school and are no longer interested in learning. School can feel pointless, even though learning should be seen as an adventure and not a chore.

3. It Can Cause Damage to a Child's Social Development

Science has revealed that exposing kids to anger can disrupt their social development and have long-term consequences. When your reaction to your child is harsh and inappropriate, their developing brain circuits get disrupted. This problem affects how they relate with people as well as how they solve everyday problems. Their ability to interact with people is impacted, and they have less control over regulating their behaviors.

Your child starts gaining a greater awareness of their individuality at a young age. Their sense of self in the early stages sets the pattern for the rest of their life. This early stage is when they develop friendships, understand people's thoughts and beliefs, listen when others speak, initiate play, and create games.

However, the effect of your anger may impair their social development. They could stop showing interest in playing with other kids. They might become rigid with their routines and get upset when things change. They won't realize they are doing something wrong when they won't share or take turns with other kids.

4. It Can Cause Damage to Your Parent-Child Relationship

Have you ever thought about your future relationship with your children? What do you dream your future will be like with your kids?

The anger you have now can damage the relationship you have later with your child. They've soaked in the negative emotions you've dispersed and may deal with their problems without your help.

If they don't know how to effectively express themselves and handle complicated feelings, they'll hold on to those emotions until they explode. Your kids will build an emotional wall to prevent others from hurting them. This barrier is detrimental to your parent-child relationship because your child won't let their guard down. As a result, they'll pull away without an opportunity to make peace with you.

I met a girl a few years ago who wasn't in contact with her parents because she believed they caused her problems. When I inquired more, she revealed to me that while she was growing up, her father was indifferent to the house and his children. This made the mother always annoyed and angry. There were not many family conversations and when they did talk, her parents were always shouting. Because of her experience, she assumed other families were like that.

She was always quiet when among people. She felt anxious and shy and avoided being in the public eye. After going to college, she met other people and realized that her parents had raised her in an angry environment. She finally understands why she was always anxious.

Remember, even though the days seem long, the years ahead are quite short. Each stage of your child's development presents its unique opportunities and challenges.

Parents that encourage their child's emotional development in healthy ways are more likely to respond to these challenges productively.

Every day is a new day and an opportunity to turn things around with your kids. Why not seize the opportunity now? In the next chapter, we'll discuss practical strategies for getting your kids to listen to you (instead of driving you nuts!).

leave a review

I hope you're enjoying my book and ask if you can spare
a quick moment to write a review or hit the star rating
to help me keep going. Thank you for your help.

SCAN ME

PART 3

EFFECTIVE PARENTING STRATEGIES

CHAPTER 7

HOW TO GET KIDS TO LISTEN WITHOUT YELLING

"Yelling silences your message. Speak quietly so your children can hear your words instead of just your voice."

— L.R. Knost

Many of us see yelling as the best option when our kids misbe-have. It feels like a natural response, and most parents have done it. But does it really work? Does it create the kind of change you want to see in your kids?

If we're truthful with ourselves, we'll all agree that yelling changes little to nothing about how our kids behave. It can even escalate a simple situation rather than help.

When we yell at our kids, they're at higher risk for psychological ef-fects. The main problem with yelling is that many parents have gotten more used to communicating this way instead of calmly speaking with their child. Frequent yelling registers in a child's brain. As a result, they expect their parents to yell about even the slightest issue.

We've discussed what anger entails, and we've defined who's responsible for anger problems between parents and kids. Now, we'll focus on seeking solutions to our anger. This chapter discusses effective ways to get our kids to listen to us *without* yelling.

How to Stop Yelling at Your Child

To a large extent, how you approach a situation determines your child's reaction. If you start calmly, you have a better chance of them listening to you. But if you approach the situation when you're already in a bad mood, you're more likely to be triggered. Your child will sense the tension and may act out.

Learn how to speak appropriately to your kids, including how to maintain a peaceful tone. A simple way to accomplish this is to learn what triggers your emotions, no matter how many they are.

Let's do a quick exercise. Grab a paper and pen. Now, start writing down all of your child's behaviors that make you mad. Which of these behaviors make your blood boil?

Refer to Chapter Two to help you identify and understand your possible triggers. If you know these triggers ahead of time, you can work to keep them from controlling you. The following are strategies you can use to stop yelling at your child.

1. Be respectful to your kids

Respectfully telling your children what you *want* them to do is more effective than screaming what you *don't* want them to do. This method is not only applicable to communicating with children but with everyone.

You can be respectful by acknowledging that your child isn't a bad person but that the behavior isn't good. Respect your child as a human and stop making them feel bad about themselves.

Avoid conveying blame, shame, or pain to them. Doing so isn't helpful, as it can make them feel worse and even embarrassed around people. They could become aggressive or develop low self-esteem, ultimately preventing them from having healthy relationships with others.

Even though it may look like you're achieving results quickly by yelling, doing so does more harm than good. For example, pretend your child walks in with a failed test result while you're having a conversation with your friend. Rather than scolding your child in the friend's presence, leave the situation for later.

If you shame your child in front of your friend, your child will most likely shut down. They may find it difficult to be comfortable in the presence of that particular person and even others that come around.

Another example is when you have a family member over for dinner and your child doesn't use good etiquette while eating. You can point out the misbehavior and calmly correct him instead of embarrassing him with criticisms like, *"How old are you?"*, *" How many times do I have to tell you that?"*, or *"Why can't you do anything right?"*

Imagine someone close to you saying these same things to you. Wouldn't you feel hurt?

Let's take ourselves as an example. What if you have friends over for dinner and your husband makes a negative remark about your appearance, saying you don't look attractive because you didn't wash your hair or only wear pajamas at home. How would you feel?

Wouldn't you feel disrespected and embarrassed? I'm guessing you'd feel so ashamed that you'd stop the conversation and want dinner to be over as soon as possible.

That's exactly how your child feels when you do something similar! Embarrassing your child will only make things worse.

2. Give a related consequence

It's important to set consequences that fit your child's misbehaviors. Example consequences could be taking away privileges, as long as they're reasonable in duration. For example, *"No phones at the dinner table. If you bring your phone, you won't be allowed to use your phone for one week."*

This way, the consequence is suited to the misbehavior. You're being reasonable by depriving them of their phone for one week. However, taking away their phone for a month for bringing it to the dining table may be overstretching it, which can make your actions ineffective.

Another example is stopping them from playing video games for a whole month because they didn't do homework. This may not be as effective as asking them to only play at specified hours. You know your child's capabilities. Setting expectations above their level will cause them to fail.

Know the consequences that work for your child, and remember that what works for one child may not work for another.

3. Consistently follow through

It isn't enough to just set consequences for your kid's actions and wait for the results. You need to consistently check up on how they're doing. Follow-throughs are not only important for misbehavior but good behavior as well. This way, kids can see that there's a reward for doing the right thing.

If they've done well, you can praise them, give hugs, or simply pat their back. However, if they misbehave, follow through by doing exactly what you said you would.

An example of a good follow-through is delaying a privilege your kids normally get. Consider taking away certain privileges like:

- Their favorite ice cream because they refused to brush their teeth
- Keeping them from playing video games for a week because they disrespected you
- Restricting various other activities they like

This way, your kid will try to solve the puzzle of what they did wrong and try not to do it again. Ensure the consequence fits the misdeed.

As parents who have so much to do in so little time, we tend to forget some of the things we say. In the same regard, we forget to enforce the negative consequences we promised. You may not always notice, but your kids are closely watching and know when you haven't taken action as promised. Over time, it will register in their minds that you don't do what you say, and they will be encouraged to misbehave.

4. Set expectations

Explain the consequences of breaking the rules to your child early on. Make your consequences known so that you can establish expectations. For example, when you say something like, *"If you don't do your assignments, there will be no watching TV for a week,"* your child already knows they'll lose access to their favorite TV show if they don't do their assignments. Most kids would rather do the assignment than lose such privileges.

Let your children know what behaviors are acceptable at home or outside and which ones aren't. The best way to do this is by timing your corrections properly and ensuring consequences happen immediately. For example, as soon as the child misbehaves, tell them on the spot if they are alone with you. If you've given a prior warning, enforce the consequence immediately.

Use calm and subtle words. Instead of starting the conversation with *"You never"* or *"You always,"* start with **"I've noticed."** This way, you're getting into a problem-solving state of mind.

Don't say, *"You never listen to me,"* or *"You always cause problems."* Instead, start with, *"I've noticed you didn't pay attention to my words "* or *"I've noticed we've had some issues with... "* Stating the concern clearly can give your child the opportunity to explain their actions.

5. Ask your child to repeat back the rule

Ensure your child always repeats the rule you've set. You can also ask them to repeat the consequences to ensure there's an understanding between you both. Don't forget that you're dealing with kids. There's no better way to confirm that it has registered in their mind than with a verbal confirmation.

Having them repeat what you say can help improve communication between the two of you. Instead of demanding, *"Repeat what I say!"* a better alternative is, *"Sweetheart, repeat after me"* in a soft but affirmative voice. This way, they're more likely to listen and will be more cooperative.

In the same way that kids learn the letters of the alphabet by reciting them, you can make them repeat your instructions and rules after you. This gives them the opportunity to personalize the rules for themselves.

Simple No-Yelling Checklist

We all want to be good parents. We aim to be parents who don't need to yell, scream, get angry, or even hit their kids. However, we need to understand that stopping these actions depends on our self-awareness.

The following are three simple ways to become more aware and mindful of yourself so that you stop yelling and live peacefully with your kids.

1. Check Your Language

Kids thrive on positive words and are often happy-go-lucky. But they also experience the occasional blues, especially when hurt by words.

As author Yehuda Berg says, *"Words are singularly the most powerful force available to humanity... Words have energy and power with the ability to help, to heal, to hurt, to harm, to humiliate, and to humble."*

Words are the smallest unit of a language, and even the smallest of them carry great power. The words you choose and how you use them can either build your child's confidence or tear it down. Your child learns everything they know by observing the people around them. Therefore, it's important to check your language and use positive words with your kids.

What kind of words do you use for your child? Are your words harsh? Cruel? Sarcastic? Degrading? Abusive?

Here are things you should *never* say to your children. If your words are anything like these, you need to watch your language and try to use more positive words when speaking to your children.

- *Shut up*
- *You're stupid*

- *Don't talk to me like that*
- *Stop talking to me*
- *Why can't you be more like your sister/brother?*
- *I wish you were never born*
- *No one cares*
- *Can't you do anything right?*
- *I'm ashamed that you are my child*
- *You are the most difficult child ever*
- *You're such a disappointment*

2. Check Your Thoughts and Own Behavior

As humans, we've hardwired certain thoughts and behaviors. When you're aware of your thoughts and behaviors, you can manage them more effectively and find that you don't need to yell at your kids. The way you think influences your behavior, so it's crucial to check your thoughts. When you get triggered by your child, it's time to do some soul searching. Turn the lens on yourself and explore what has caused those triggers.

To check your thoughts and behaviors, you need a pen and notebook/diary to track them. You'll be answering some questions to help you make the most of the exercise.

Write down your answers to the questions below in your notebook:

- How do you speak to your children? In a soft or angry tone of voice?
- Are there situations where you spank your child?
- Can you think of a situation that makes you think negatively?
- How has this particular thought/belief made you feel? Rate the feeling from 1 to 10, with 10 being the worst.
- How can you reframe this thought? Think of a kinder thought and write it down.

That's it! Simple right?

Engage in this exercise as much as you like throughout the day. By writing them down, you give your thoughts new and more positive power. With enough practice, you'll train yourself to automatically reframe negative thoughts and behaviors without even thinking about it.

3. Check Your Self-Regulation

How do you approach a tense situation with your child? Is your manner calm and confident? Do you set limits using kindness regardless of how your child reacts?

What if your child is argumentative and showing anger? Can you remain composed and calm?

As a parent, monitoring your ability to self-regulate can help you choose how to react to situations. For example, while you may think that life is unfair, self-pity and blaming yourself don't matter in the end. Instead, how you react to the situation is what matters.

But how can you self-regulate?

- **By recognizing that you have three options in every situation.** You can either approach, attack, or avoid a situation. It is important that you make the right choice for every situation.
- **By becoming aware of your fleeting feelings.** Do you prefer to run away from a difficult situation, or do you always lash out at your child for triggering you?
- **By monitoring your body.** This will help you get clues about your feelings when they're not immediately obvious. For example, it can be a panic attack, shaky hands, a red face, or an increased heart rate.

Self-regulation requires time, commitment, and practice. Align your thoughts and behaviors with your goals and then make the necessary changes. Work and life are generally stressful, but it's important to self-regulate so you're in control over your response in difficult times. Some ways of self-regulating are meditating, exercising, keeping a journal, seeking feedback from friends, practicing self-compassion, and forming positive affirmations.

Finally, no matter how difficult your relationship with your kid is, this chapter will be useful. That's even if you're currently arguing, or engaging in a yelling match with your kids daily. The steps we've discussed will help save your sanity and relationship with your kids. In the next chapter, we'll discuss the self-reflection process so you can know where problems come from, what solutions don't work, and how to parent peacefully.

CHAPTER 8

PARENTING METHODS THAT WORK

"Without self-awareness, we are as babies in the cradles."

— Virginia Woolf

When starting your motherhood journey, you never imagined you'd be yelling and spanking your kids when they misbehave. These are your precious and innocent cuties we're talking about! Why would the idea ever cross your mind? However, when your baby becomes a preschooler, the real struggle starts. At this point, your child starts testing your patience and pushing buttons you didn't know you had.

This was my everyday experience years ago. I was constantly arguing with a little person who wasn't listening to me. He was being rude, treating me badly, and acting irresponsibly, and I was becoming frustrated and depressed. This pattern continued until I researched and found parenting methods that truly work!

Before I unveil them, let's start with what *doesn't* work.

What Doesn't Work

If you're having a difficult time trying to be a good parent and having a peaceful relationship with your kids, you need to look at **yourself** first. This step will help you figure out where the problem comes from. Next, you need to identify ineffective strategies you're currently using and find more effective ones. Unfortunately, not knowing what you're doing wrong will keep you in an angry cycle, and you'll just keep repeating those mistakes.

What can you do instead? First, we'll be discussing the actions many parents take that don't work.

1. Yelling Doesn't Work

As parents, we have many ways of influencing our children's behaviors and encouraging them to do what we want. Yelling is part of them. However, we need to understand that even though yelling seems like the quickest response, it is ineffective because it transmits the wrong message to our kids.

None of us likes being yelled at, especially kids. It makes them feel embarrassed, demeaned, and scared. If you're looking for an effective way to change your child's behavior, yelling shouldn't be part of it, period. When you make your child feel scared and embarrassed, they automatically enter fight-or-flight mode, and the learning center of their brain starts to shut down.

If this happens, your child can't learn or listen to your words. When you yell, their brain tells them you are a threat. It automatically shuts down the other parts of the brain meant for protecting the child.

There are many other reasons why yelling won't work for your child. If you have a yelling match with them, you show them that you're at odds with each other. In other words, you make it clear to them that you aren't on their team. Kids wind up feeling defensive, confused, and disconnected from their parents. They won't be receptive to your guidance or open about problems. Yelling can ruin the connection you have with your child.

If you yell at your kids, it produces similar results to physical punishment, making them feel stressed. Their anxiety and depression levels increase which can lead to behavioral issues. Obviously, this shows that we aren't getting our desired results from yelling.

When you yell at your kids, you don't look authoritative to them. In fact, what it does is make you look weak like you can't stay in control in front of your kids. If you're honest with yourself, you'll agree with me that you yell because you are weak. If you had things under control, you wouldn't need to yell. It is at this moment when kids don't listen to you, respect you, or carry out simple instructions. Their bad behaviors get to you, and you show your weakness by yelling.

In essence, yelling is the response you give when you're confused about what to do.

Parents need to understand that yelling won't work for kids, even if it seems like it can get a quick response. That response results from fear, and it won't be sustained.

However, knowing that some methods of changing a child's behavior are more effective than others, it is your responsibility as parents to pursue a better course of action. Adopt a method that truly works instead of being an angry and scary parent that's always yelling.

2. Spanking Doesn't Work

Nope! It doesn't! While spanking may seem like a disciplinary tool to get your kid to listen to you, it doesn't work. It only sends a message to your child stating, *"I want you to behave so that I can feel calmer,"* or *"I don't know how to stay calm unless you behave the way I want you to."*

Spanking your child is very bad in itself. It's what people do when they don't know what else to do. Have you ever wondered why you spank your kids? I'm guessing you spank them for the same reasons every day. Maybe they don't put their clothes away even though you warned them countless times not to throw them on the floor.

Perhaps they talk back, use bad language, or hit their siblings. But does spanking really work? Do you see any long-term good results for your disciplinary action?

For many years now, spanking has been adopted as a normal way to discipline a child. But studies have revealed that spanking has harmful effects on children. In fact, spanking is now seen as a form of physical abuse on kids.

How can you justify spanking your child? What does it do?

Perhaps your parents carried out the same punishment when you were a kid. You may have been told that it's an acceptable way of correcting behavior. But, after many years of doing it, you're still seeing no results except adverse effects. How then can you stop doing something you've gotten so used to? How can you stop your child from engaging in the annoying, dangerous, and bad behaviors they keep doing but without spanking them?

No doubt, spanking can give quick results, much like yelling. But prepare yourself because more is coming. Get ready to have a more aggressive child, one who's filled with rage towards you, their siblings, friends at school, and their partner later on.

Also, be prepared to have a child that exhibits antisocial behaviors.

If you keep spanking your child, they'll feel devalued. They may develop a low sense of self-worth and depression. In addition, this drastic action can end up backfiring because it encourages them to lie. While trying to escape physical pain, your child will become desperate to avoid being spanked and lying even though they know they shouldn't.

When you spank your kids, you show them that violence is the right way to solve a problem. In recent years, there's been a significant social focus on bullying. Spanking your child can be seen as bullying. You're also teaching your child that spanking is an effective way of getting others to do certain things. For example, tapping your child's hand hard or giving them a quick swat on their behind can send your child messages indicating that physical hurt is a great way to get someone's attention and correct inappropriate behaviors.

Since children learn things by looking up to their parents and modeling them, spanking gives the message that hitting someone is an appropriate way of expressing feelings and solving a problem. But all your child can learn from spanking is, *"I understand that she'll spank me if she's here while I do something I'm not supposed to. But I can misbehave now since she isn't here."* Because of this thinking, they will be more likely to object to your request, especially when you aren't there to inflict the pain.

When you spank your child, you aren't building a positive relationship with your child. A child will avoid a parent that spanks. They won't want to spend time with them or talk to them. At one point, I noticed that my son wanted to spend more time with his friends in school rather than with me. He avoided going out with me and would prefer to lock himself indoors than come out of his room and talk to me.

I finally realized that spanking isn't a solution. If we want our kids to behave, it's best to try and understand them. Give them reasons to do the right thing, and share the consequences for not doing them. You should aim to build a good relationship with your kid instead of spanking them.

What Does Work

Now that you know what doesn't work with your kids, it's time to discuss what works so that you can start applying them.

1. Self-Awareness is Key

As a parent, I've always struggled with carrying out this role peacefully, and for many years, it caused emotional distress for both my son and myself. I was in full survival mode, focusing on my 9-to-5 job, working hard, and providing the basic needs for my family. Even though I was a dedicated mom who loved her son, I didn't feel at peace.

Sadly, many of us weren't taught how to be self-aware when we were younger. As a result, we often make the same mistakes our parents did because we lack the right tools to prevent history from repeating itself.

Let's first examine what self-awareness is.

According to psychologist Shelley Duval, *"Self-awareness is the capacity to recognize your own feelings, behaviors, and characteristics—to understand your cognitive, physical and emotional self."*

I like to think of awareness as the act of paying attention and being honest with yourself.

With self-awareness, you can make more intentional choices. The logic behind self-awareness is simple. The more self-aware you become, the more likely you are to behave in ways that are consistent with who you want to be. You're more likely to be happy with how you interact with the people in your life: your kids, partner, and friends.

Now that you know what self-awareness is, let me ask:

Have you explored your self-awareness today? Do you feel like exploring it tomorrow?

You may not know it yet, but self-awareness is a powerful anger management tool that can change your life.

If you're more self-aware, you can connect with your kids better. Parents without self-awareness can get caught up in their emotions when they are supposed to be present with their kids. They might not also know when they are reliving the same experience they had with their parents. They'll unknowingly repeat the same childhood patterns.

Sometimes, self-awareness entails knowing that you don't have the capacity to do certain things, and when you know this, you can focus on other things you are capable of doing.

2. Recognizing Self-Awareness

How do you become self-aware? How can you recognize whether you've become self-aware?

For me, it was only a few years ago that I could recognize my self-awareness. I was juggling the tasks of being a mom and working full-time. While I had spent some time identifying my strengths and weaknesses as a mom, I didn't recognize what self-awareness was.

Until I had to navigate through my emotions and the situations that caused them, I concluded that I needed to be more self-aware. I began to recognize when and why I was always feeling frustrated, sad, and angry. This knowledge helped build my confidence to use healthy coping strategies as I dealt with strong and overwhelming emotions.

I know I'm not alone. Many parents also express their emotions impulsively and fail to realize why they're angry or upset. However, if we want to turn things around, we need to recognize the importance of acknowledging our emotions, even after the fact. The issue is that we often forget why we felt that way in the first place, making it difficult to find suitable coping strategies that work.

3. Learning Conscious Parenting

As a parent with a full-time job that takes much of my time, it usually feels like I have no energy at the end of the day. It's difficult to cater to my family in the way that I'd like. After dealing with work demands, my only wish is to come home and rest.

However, the reality is that life at home can be stressful as well. It can even be more overwhelming than life at work. Sadly, our kids are at the receiving end of our stress.

If this is similar to your situation, how then can we ensure that our stressful day doesn't affect our kids? How can we keep our bad mood from affecting our kids? The answer may lie in conscious parenting.

When you hear/see the word "consciousness," what's the first thing that comes to mind? Does it sound like a sense of awareness? Being alert? Or a state of being fully awake?

If so, you're already more familiar with what conscious parenting means than you know.

According to conscious parenting expert Eric Morrison at Columbia University, *"Conscious parenting is a parent-focused, connection-based parenting approach where the parent uses self-awareness to develop a strong, authentic connection to their child."*

The idea of conscious parenting suggests that instead of striving to fix your child, you should rather look inward. If you practice conscious parenting, you see your kids as independent beings that can teach you to become more self-aware even though they are still growing and developing. In addition, by being a conscious parent, you are intentional about the parenting decisions you make.

You may wonder why you need to start with your own behavior when it's your *kids* that are misbehaving. First, you need to recognize that your life experience dictates why and how you do the things you do, especially when it comes to raising your kids.

As I mentioned in the earlier chapters, many of us repeat the patterns we learned from our parents. What's even more unsettling is that our childhood traumas influence our decision-making process without even knowing it.

Conscious Parenting: The Way To Be A Better Parent

By being a conscious parent, you've worked to confront your fears and given up on the superficial expectations for your kids. You've realized that your kids are not here to meet your needs, and they can't take away your pain.

You already know how your childhood experiences and culture have conditioned you, and you don't need to impose these on your kids. Instead, you allow your kids to be their authentic selves by getting rid of these learned ideas.

As a conscious parent, you need to allow your kids to discover the world for themselves and draw their conclusions. Don't always try to be in control.

You're a role model for your kids. Why should you allow them to discover the world themselves? Doesn't that sound contradictory?

No, it doesn't. It means you need to be mindful of how you paint the picture of the world to your kids. Even though you are their parents and they learn everything about the world from you, it would help if you could step back and allow them to develop their own ideas. Even if their process doesn't make sense to you or you think you can help them "paint a better picture." Allow them to experience it themselves.

You don't need to be the perfect parent. Of course, it's not easy to avoid making mistakes. But at the very least, you need to be aware of yourself, your words, and your behaviors towards your kids. You need to do your best not to transfer your personal expectations, issues, and pain to them. You'll accidentally transfer some mental baggage, no doubt. However, be aware of when you are doing this. Check in with yourself and alter your actions.

But why conscious parenting? Does it really help?

Have you ever said something and realized you sounded exactly like your mom or dad, in a bad way? That's a very good reason you need to start practicing conscious parenting. If, while growing up, your parents allowed their own issues, fears, and negative conditioning to interfere with their parenting style, you shouldn't let that be the case for your relationship with your kids.

Many parents have unconsciously unloaded their past experiences on their children, which has made their relationship with their kids hellish. That was my situation until I began a journey of self-discovery. I uncovered my negative patterns and became more aware of the reason I did certain things. I now notice when I transfer my problems to my son. When this happens, I immediately regroup and fix the error.

As you practice this approach, you will realize that you are becoming less defensive and reactive than you were in the past. You'll start to see things more objectively, creating space for better responses instead of harsh reactions.

Of course, it takes time to become a conscious parent. However, with constant practice, you'll stop yourself when you do or say something you shouldn't. Before you make one of these mistakes, stop and think, *"I really don't want to hurt my child with such mean words,"* or *"I should say something helpful rather than putting my child down."* What you are doing here is realigning your words!

Parents need to set clear boundaries and be consistent with communicating them. Examples of these types of boundaries are riding bikes with helmets on, not running in the parking lot, and not watching TV right before bedtime. You need to make them non-negotiable.

Key Elements Of Conscious Parenting

- Conscious parenting entails letting go of your ego, personal conditioning, attachments, desires, and wishes.
- Parenting isn't a one-way transmission process. It's a two-way relationship involving a parent and child.
- Rather than giving out serious consequences for minor issues, parents need to create boundaries and use positive reinforcement early on.
- Rather than force certain "good" behaviors on kids, parents should focus on getting their own behaviors right. These include expectations, language, and self-regulation.
- Parents shouldn't assume that parenting is just about making a child happy. As kids become teenagers, they face struggles.

Parents' needs and egos shouldn't be forgotten because of a child's growth.

- Showing acceptance means parents are present and engaged in whatever situations present themselves.

So far, we've discussed ineffective parenting approaches. We also discussed how self-awareness is the key to peaceful parenting. In the next chapter, we'll discuss more effective parenting strategies and explore ways for you to keep your cool when the kids push your buttons.

CHAPTER 9

HOW TO KEEP YOUR COOL WHEN KIDS PUSH YOUR BUTTONS

"Because children grow up, we think a child's purpose is to grow up. But a child's purpose is to be a child."

— Tom Stoppard

The pressures of life are numerous. They range from things we forgot to do until the last minute, arriving late for appointments, and financial and health worries. The list is endless. While struggling with our own stress, our kids add theirs to the mix. They refuse to unglue themselves from the TV and do their homework. They tease their siblings and won't touch anything on their plate at dinner. Almost all parents would lose their cool if they had to deal with these situations by themselves.

We usually get upset when kids aren't doing what we want. We start worrying that we aren't doing a great job as parents. This doubt surfaces because we are unsure of what to do to get our kids under control. The thought of the future is scary because we can't imagine living the rest of our lives like this. As a result, our anxiety increases. An effective solution here is to prepare ahead of time. Know that your kids will push your buttons and when they do, you shouldn't take it personally. Kids will always be kids, and as parents, our job is to stay calm and guide them.

But how do you stay cool and avoid worsening the situation? This chapter will provide effective strategies for parents struggling to regulate their emotions. You'll learn how to stay cool when your kids push your buttons.

7 Effective Tips For Staying Cool

It was 10:00 pm, and my son was still on the phone. This happened after I set a rule that there would be no electronics used after 9:30 pm. So when I peeped into his room and saw him on the phone, I reminded him nicely of the rule and asked him to put the phone down as we'd agreed. He ignored me. So I reminded him again.

Eventually, I raised my voice and made him stop. I said goodnight and thought that was it, assuming he had gone to bed.

A couple of hours later, just in case, I quietly opened his door and saw him watching YouTube under the blanket. It was already past midnight! This made me blow up and I felt betrayed. My son had disrespected me. Of course, any parent would be upset and lose their cool if not careful.

When I calmly asked him to stop, he waved at me to go away. And that was it! My buttons were pushed. Immediately, I exploded.

He knew exactly what button to push and tested my limit until I blew up. No matter how hard I tried to remain calm that night, I just couldn't. I really tried, but I got to my breaking point.

This experience became constant, and I reminded myself that even though I had a breaking point (we all do), I wouldn't allow it to define me. Instead, I sought help and got working on strategies to remain cool even when my son misbehaved.

And here comes some good news!

The following are the best strategies you can apply when your child pushes *your* button. These strategies take a little bit of practice, but over time, you'll get through even big issues without yelling or getting frustrated.

1. Recognize That You're Getting Annoyed

Even if you're one of the nicest parents in the world, you can't escape being annoyed at times. You don't need to be a mean parent to put your child on edge. Now that you know you can't prevent the problem completely, knowing *when* you're getting annoyed can reduce the intense emotions.

Annoyance can be hard to pinpoint. Sometimes it's hidden. We usually don't notice it until we've reached the dark side. However, if we stop and observe ourselves, we'll notice when the annoyance is building. This way, we can quickly do something about it before our emotions get out of control.

When you feel like your buttons have been pushed, consider why you think you are right and your child is wrong. In other words, don't react to the idea that your child is automatically wrong.

Some signs of annoyance include teeth grinding, body shakes, fast-beating heart, anxiety, sweating, pacing, irritability, yelling, etc.

If you can acknowledge that you are annoyed and identify your other emotions, this is your first step to understanding your emotions and maintaining your cool.

2. Stop And Breathe

This next step can still be used even when you've gone down the wrong path and are already yelling. Immediately, you'll notice the feeling of annoyance or anger. Don't follow through. Stop. Treat the feeling like a red light. When it appears, you immediately need to stop your car. This feeling should serve as a STOP sign for you.

Immediately after the sign appears, drop everything you are doing and close your mouth, even if you're in the middle of a sentence. You can even repeat a mantra like *"Everything will be fine," "I can handle it better this time," "I can be a peaceful mom,"* or *"I'm a loving mom, not an angry mom."* As you recite the mantra, keep breathing slowly until you feel calmness flowing within you. This simple exercise will give you a small pause between action and thought, allowing you to choose wisely.

You shouldn't be embarrassed to do this. You're only modeling a good anger management technique, so save the awkward feeling for when your child's tantrum occurs.

3. Count to Five

This is another strategy that encourages parents to wait to address the issue with their children instead of doing it while they are angry. Remaining calm when faced with adversity will allow parents to re-center so they can talk reasonably with their child.

You should be familiar with the counting to 5 strategies before you take any action. The approach emphasizes two elements of anger management: time and distraction. As you are busy counting, you distract yourself from adding fuel to your anger. In addition, your breathing counteracts the fight or flight response beneath your anger. This practice should bring a sense of relaxation as you learn to control your initial impulses and help you become more self-aware.

Now start counting 1 to 5 and take a big breath. Don't count quickly, count slowly. The purpose of counting is to give you some space to separate yourself from the situation. As you count, don't allow your thoughts to distract you. Remain focused on your breath as you are breathing in and out. You should feel better within a few seconds.

4. Listen To Your Body Response

Listening to your body means considering your body's responses to a situation. On bad days, we often feel stiffness, aches, pains, or soreness and assume these ailments are random. Perhaps you think you are simply aging. Maybe you assume it is genetics or you are meant to feel that way. Then on easy parenting days, you beam with energy and assume it's just your lucky day.

Well, luck doesn't have anything to do with it.

You don't need to try concealing your anger by listening to your body's responses. Instead, it would help if you *resisted* acting on your anger when you feel it. You can do this by noticing the anger in you. Feel the suffocating sensation in your throat and the tightness in your belly. Notice yourself clenching your fists or how fast your heart races. Take note of your shoulders tightening and your sudden, shallow breathing.

Notice these sorts of body responses. This will help you catch your anger quicker and allow you to stay calm.

5. Change Your Thoughts

Changing your thoughts is an effective way to reduce your anger and maintain your cool. If you keep thinking negatively about situations, people, and events, you can easily get caught up in overwhelming emotions. You're less likely to experience anger when you change these thoughts.

Our thinking patterns are habitual, but we can replace our negative thoughts with positive ones with a little self-awareness and some practice. We need to reframe our thoughts about certain situations so we can experience different feelings. For example, if you think you need to punish your child severely, you'll only feel angrier. Instead, remind yourself that you are dealing with a child who is acting their age.

Understand that they need your love, especially when they do not act like they deserve it. Be willing to move away from anger.

6. Empathize

Empathizing is when you understand someone's experience to the extent of imagining yourself having the same experience. By being empathetic, you show understanding and kindness. It will help your relationship with your child if you understand their experiences, needs, and feelings.

Start listening to your child's feelings and try to see things from their point of view. As adults, parents tend to only focus on their adult perspective. But remember that you have a tiny human who will eventually become an adult someday. They're just a kid now. Put yourself in their shoes and think about a time you wished your parents would've reacted differently when you were angry. When it would've felt nice for your mom to listen to you. Maybe you wished she'd have expressed her love by saying she understood you.

When you feel empathy towards your child, you're also helping them feel better about themselves. You remind them that they aren't alone in their issues and you are there to share their feelings, thoughts, and emotions.

7. Practice, Practice, and Practice!

I need to be honest with you. Keeping your cool is one of the hardest things any parent or anyone in general can do. For parents who easily fly off the handle, it will be even more difficult because you are teaching your brain a new way to be disciplined.

This process requires lots of practice. The good news is that whenever you resist the urge to act on your anger, you are rewiring your brain. This makes managing your anger easier with every attempt.

You will lose your cool sometimes, but if you keep practicing, noticing your emotions, and treating yourself with compassion, you will find it easier to stay cool when your child acts up. You may even notice that you rarely lose your temper anymore. No doubt, you will still experience some childish behaviors since you live with kids. But this time, you will have a reaction that involves more love and less drama.

Learning To Be A Calm Parent

Being in control of your emotions and reactions and eventually becoming a peaceful parent may seem far-fetched, especially when your kids misbehave. But how exactly can you remain calm when your child is talking back, screaming at you, slamming the door, or throwing things? It's very easy for your self-control to go through the roof within seconds when faced with such behavior.

You're worried about lots of things as a parent: your kids' safety, their success in school, their health, peer pressure, bullies, and the list goes on. As a parent, you are doing all you can to raise a healthy and successful child, and what do you get in return? Your child acts as if you're their worst enemy! Situations like these can make any parent feel overwhelmed. Sometimes, you may even start giving up on the idea of a "happily ever after" because it seems like your dream of peaceful parenting will never come true.

What can you do then? How can you be a peaceful parent? You are one step closer to your answer! The following strategies are helpful ways to parent peacefully even during trouble. These strategies don't just focus on surface-level behavior but touch on the underlying emotions.

1. Manage Your Emotions

Sometimes, it can feel like our emotions came out of nowhere, adding to the tiredness we already feel as parents. In these moments, managing our emotions can prove difficult.

There are two ways to respond to our emotions: acting on them or suppressing them. If you act when experiencing strong emotions like anger, you can easily create unfavorable consequences for your relationship with your child. Acting on anger can provoke even more intense emotions, leading to further issues.

Suppressing emotions is more dangerous because no matter how hard you try holding them in, they will find their way out, causing more damage. Therefore, it is important to learn to manage your emotions.

To be a peaceful parent, you need to learn how to respond calmly to situations instead of overreacting. Learning this process may take time, depending on your personality and family background.

However, remember that you are human, and you can learn just about anything.

The human brain isn't fixed. It produces stimuli that continue to mold the brain's chemistry. By meditating, journaling, and exercising, the brain can be reshaped. Knowing what sets you off can help you to respond differently.

2. Connect With Your Child

Playing with your child can seem impossible when you're always busy and feel tired at the end of the day. However, you need to keep in mind that having a connection with your child is what makes parenting fun and worth it. Imagine the beautiful smile on your child's face when they feel you love them. Don't you want to experience that joy?

Many parents don't share the same idea of fun that their kids do. For example, your child may enjoy dancing, and since you don't know how to dance, you want to avoid it. But as parents who want to connect with their kids, you need to find ways to engage with them. That might mean dancing with them and having fun while doing it!

Connection is also important for kids who want to do what their parents expect and are open to learning from them. It's a good feeling for our kids to know that their parents are proud of them. Having a positive family experience will also help them form healthy relationships with others as they grow.

Ensure you make time each day to play and connect with your child. Allow him to unload any emotions they may be carrying because there are times when their emotions may feel so overwhelming, and they want to cry and let them all out. When you are with your child, be more self-aware and focus on the experience. Postpone calling someone or chatting on social media; be there for both of you.

3. Emotional Coaching

How can your child learn to do better if you find it difficult to regulate your emotions? Don't forget that your child looks up to you and mirrors your actions. Introduce the concept of emotional coaching to your child. This will help teach them that some behaviors are unacceptable although feeling emotions is part of being a human.

For example, it is okay to feel angry, but it is inappropriate to express or show your anger by kicking things, yelling, or punching the wall. You need to instruct your child on the right way to deal with emotions. Alert them to the times they aren't regulating their emotions, such as when they're throwing something, hitting someone, or screaming when they need something.

Children don't know how to handle and process their emotions. When they feel threatened, they can easily lash out. It is up to you to teach them. Model the right behavior for them, as you are your child's emotional coach. This way, you can show them right from wrong.

CHAPTER 10

ANGER STRATEGIES FOR EVERYDAY PROBLEMS

"Anger doesn't solve anything. It builds nothing but it can destroy everything."

— Lawrence Douglas Wilder

While the anger-filled situations we face with our kids daily may not be serious, they are enough to irritate us.

Let's assume you are on a diet. It would be wise to calculate the calories in your food and to eat fewer carbohydrates since they make you gain weight. What you're doing here is intentionally choosing what to eat and what not to eat. It means you're thinking about your situation and finding a way out of it. You may not always succeed, but your diet is more effective when you are intentional about it.

The same thing is true when it comes to parenting. If you know what to do and what not to do in certain situations, you can avoid becoming overly angry. This strategy may not *always* be effective, but it will help prevent the situation from getting worse.

In this chapter, we take one step further into our journey of becoming a peaceful parent. Here, I discuss eight common angry situations to give you a clear idea of how each scenario plays out. I share tips on what to do and what not to do to manage each type of situation. This is an important chapter I want you to pay attention to because it discusses everyday experiences using practical examples.

Let's get started!

1. Backtalk

We all know how upsetting kids talking back to us can be. When it happens, we feel immediate alarm: Our kids can't talk to us that way! This feeling is like a fireball consuming our hearts. The emotions can be unbearable, making it easy to lose our cool and overreact when it happens.

When this happens, you need to be clear on what's an acceptable level of anger. Set limits for how high these anger levels can reach. Do this so you don't blow the situation out of proportion. If you overreact, it means you are giving your child more power than they should wield. As parents, you need to make your kids follow the rules, not focus on them accepting the logic of your decisions.

Example 1:

Child: *"Can I stay out until 10:00 pm tonight?"*

Parent: *"No, don't forget you have to get up early tomorrow for soccer practice."*

Child: *"Who cares? I don't need that much sleep."*

If you've had a similar conversation, it's hard not to respond to your child angrily. However, stop before you let your anger get the best of you. Further conversation with them shows that you need to defend your judgment.

What to do:

- **Do** stay calm and keep your cool rather than lashing out or overreacting.
- **Do** remain conscious of your nonverbal communication. This can help you conceal your displeasure by being aware of your facial expression.
- **Do** address the issue with your child clearly. Set the rules for next time.
- **Do** avoid reasoning with your child in the heat of the moment. This won't drive your point home.

What not to do:

- **Don't** yell or scream at your child.
- **Don't** tell your child hurtful things like *"You're a bad child"* or *"You're hopeless."*
- **Don't** punish them or give too severe consequences.

2. Disrespectful Behavior

We all want our kids to treat us and others with kindness. We want them to learn how to communicate their feelings to us without displaying disrespectful behaviors.

But in the heat of the moment, kids may start yelling, arguing, cursing, ignoring, name-calling, and refusing our requests. Behaviors like these are a wake-up call to all parents. We need to be in control of whatever situation encourages this misbehavior. We also need to set better limits for our kids.

Example 1:

Parent: *"It's getting late. Let's go home."*

Child: *"No! I want to stay at the park! You're such a boring mom. You never let me do fun things."*

Parent: *"How dare you talk to me that way?"*

Child: *"You don't care about me! You are so mean!"*

Your child tells you this after you already gave a 5-minute warning and assumed everything would go well. However, your expectations weren't met when your child chose to disrespect you. Your anger rises, and you soon become furious.

Example 2:

Parent: *"Don't forget to put your clothes away."*

Child: *"Okay, 'Madam President.'"*

Parent: *"Why are you calling me that? Is something wrong?"*

Child: *"I don't know what you are talking about!"*

Parent: *"I don't appreciate you being sarcastic and disrespectful. Please speak appropriately to me."*

Child: *"Yeah, right."* (Sarcastically).

This final response is disrespectful. Of course, you're going to feel annoyed and frustrated when this happens, but you shouldn't immediately show your displeasure.

What to do instead:

- Don't take the behavior personally since it's about them, not you. Instead, allow yourself to feel the anger and hurt (but not excessively), and be direct and clear with your child.
- Use "When/Then" statements to reframe requests positively. Use them to inform your child about what will happen after changing their behavior. For example, you can say, *"You can play with your friends outside right after you pick up all your toys from the floor,"* or *"If you can wait until I'm done on the phone, I'll answer you."*
- Give an appropriate consequence. When your child calls you names or walks out on you after telling them not to, consider their age and determine the consequence. Don't give consequences that are too much for their age to handle or ones your child won't care about.
- Avoid power struggles. If your kid has exhibited disrespectful behaviors in the past, they will still do it again. Since you know this, anticipate it and you will be prepared next time it threatens to happen.
- Use restitution to discourage disrespectful behaviors from happening again. For example, a teen child should pay or fix anything broken out of anger, or you can have them do chores for a week after disrespecting you.

What not to do:

- Don't yell back at your child.
- Don't punish or give your child any severe consequences.
- Don't give lengthy lectures to your child.

3. Mealtime Tantrums

This is common among younger kids and is actually a healthy part of their development. Don't worry! The frequency decreases as they grow. However, if your child is experiencing many extreme meltdowns that impact their daily lives, they need help.

Example 1:

Child: *"I don't want to eat this green thing! I hate asparagus. I want fries!"*

Parent: *"Eat this veggie. Asparagus is very healthy for you."*

The child then pushes the food off the table and onto the floor, shouting at the mom that they want fries.

Example 2:

Child: *"I want to sit in the same chair you use!"*

Parent: *"No, you can't do that. You need to use the high chair for kids. It's safer for you."*

The child starts crying and the resulting dinner experience is terrible.

What to do:

- Be patient. Don't be too quick to react when you get angry. Rashness isn't helpful.
- Create a happy environment at the table. You can do this by allowing moderate play during mealtimes. For example, when you serve carrots and green beans, ask your child which will crunch louder. This way, they increase their sensory

intelligence. Allow them to explore, feel, smell, and touch their food. Even though it might get messy, playing these sorts of games is a good way to explore and have fun, especially for kids who are selective about food.

- Accept age-appropriate behaviors. You know your child. If they are acting out, it may signify that they're tired or aren't feeling well. Instead of giving a harsh response, give them a break with a nap or quiet time. If you notice that they're just trying to test you, immediately draw the line.

- Remind kids of the rules you set by being clear on your mealtime do's and don'ts. Let them know you will help them remember the rules if they are having a hard time. For example, *"If you scream again, you will be excused from the table."*

What not to do:

- Don't have unrealistic expectations. Instead, know what your child can do at their age and don't expect them to grow up overnight.

- Don't force your child to eat when they're not hungry. Since toddlers can't verbally say when they are hungry or full, you won't know if they need to eat more than they already have.

4. Dawdling in kids

Kids may sometimes seem more interested in what they want to do than what you want them to do. They may dawdle, doing things like playing with their spoon before eating, watching an interesting bug when they are supposed to get in the car, or splashing water in the sink before brushing their teeth. At these times, instead of engaging in a fighting match, choose to be a role model for your kids.

Example 1:

Say you made reservations for dinner at 7:00 pm. You're rushing to leave the house to make it on time, but you discover your child isn't dressed yet, even though you told them to get dressed an hour ago. This same scenario may happen on school days as well.

What to do:

- Give specific, step-by-step directions to your child. For example, instead of asking your child, *"Ready to go?"* tell them, *"Put on your clothes and get in the car now."* You can also tell them, *"Put on your socks and come have breakfast."* This way, they are clear about exactly what they need to do.
- Give your kid an incentive to finish. For example, *"If you get in the car now, you can continue to play when you're back home."*

What not to do:

- Don't rush your child too much. Use commands like *"Come on"* and *"Hurry up"* sparingly.
- Don't create misleading patterns by repeatedly asking your kids, *"Ready?"* while you watch YouTube videos or scroll through social media. Your child may be confused when you keep saying, *"Hurry up"* but you're doing something else. It shows you aren't ready to leave the house quickly.

5. Aggression and Violence

Some kids that don't know how to express themselves better often use aggression and violence to deal with problems. They may get violent when they're disappointed, frustrated, or angry since acting this way appears to work for them. Unfortunately, misbehaving can sometimes get them what they want, and they do this to gain power at home.

The violent child won't take "*no*" for an answer and would feel powerless and frustrated when they hear it. So they hit something or even someone.

Example 1:

Two siblings are playing with their toy cars. The older one hits the younger child because he wants to play with the blue toy he's holding. This act of aggression can be upsetting for any parent to watch.

What to do:

- Respond immediately by asking the violent sibling to stop in a firm voice. Then take the child by the hands and look them in the eyes. Calmly ask, *"That hurts, do you realize?"*
- If there's too much tension in the room, you can leave the child alone until they are calm.

What not to do:

- Don't respond in a timid voice. Whatever you say should be said firmly to show that you are serious and that their behavior isn't acceptable.
- Don't give a lengthy lecture. Keep it brief.
- Don't hit back or spank your child. Be a good role model instead.

6. Lying

Catching your child lying can create feelings of betrayal, anger, and frustration. Even though lying is normal behavior in kids, it needs to be addressed.

It's not an issue of immorality or a character flaw. A child learns to tell lies as early as three years old because that's when they know you aren't a mind reader. As they grow older (4 to 6 years old), they'll get better at telling these lies. They'll rarely get caught because they now have a bigger vocabulary and are better at understanding how people think. They can match their lies with their tone of voice and facial expressions. They may also lie to avoid hurting people's feelings.

Example 1:

You could get a phone call from your child's teacher and learn your kid has missed several tests in school. When you confront him, he claims the teacher's mistake. But you realize that your child has lied to you about other things over the past few days. For example, he lied about getting his assignments done, brushing his teeth before going to school, and not hitting his siblings.

What to do:

- Focus on seeking solutions instead of assigning blame. Since he missed several tests, you should focus on finding a way he can make them up. How can you make sure they start brushing their teeth before going to school?
- Set reasonable expectations if your child lies about finishing his house chores. Try to understand that he comes home late after soccer practice, and by the time he finishes his homework, he gets tired and wants to sleep. On these days, doing all his chores may be impossible.

- Encourage your child to tell the truth. Sit down and have a conversation about the disadvantages of lying and the benefits of telling the truth. You might say, *"How do you think Dad would feel if I lied to him?"* or *"How would you feel if I deceived you?"*

What not to do:

- Stop asking questions that set your kids up for lies. For example, you notice that your little girl is wearing red lipstick and your dressing table is messed up. When you ask, *"Did you use my lipstick?"* she will be more likely to deny it. It's better to say, *"I can see that red lipstick on your mouth."*

7. Sibling Fights

All kids fight, regardless of how close they are. Even if your kids are best friends, they're going to fight sometimes. Siblings can annoy each other, but if your kids are constantly fighting, you may feel like you can't help but yell. Children will tease, taunt, and fight with each other, which can drive any parent crazy.

Example 1:

Child 1: *"Mom! She just called me stupid!"*

Child 2: *"You liar! I didn't call you that."*

Child 1: *"She did! Mom, she always does! You just never know."*

Child 2: *"You are such a baby. Spoiled brat!"*

Child 1: *"I'm not playing with you anymore. I hate you!"*

What to do:

- Identify and then solve the problem by separating the kids. Listen to each side of the story to figure out a solution that will work for both of them.
- Teach your kids how to talk, negotiate, and compromise with each other.
- When they're angry, they tend to use harsh words. It's your duty to teach them how to talk and act appropriately when they are angry with each other.
- Praise their good behaviors by saying, *"I like how you and your sibling take turns with the swing,"* or *"Wow! You are both playing together and sharing.*
- *That's really cool."* You can reward their behaviors with treats, saying something like, *"Since you both worked out the problem well, we'll be celebrating with ice cream tonight."*

What not to do:

- Don't have a favorite child. It takes two to tango, so you can't blame one child and leave the other. For example, don't say, *"Why do you always disturb your sibling's peace all the time?"* If you keep playing favorites, the other child may feel neglected and could end up feeling like a bully. This may only encourage sibling rivalry, so always be fair.
- Don't assume you can't do anything about the situation. When there's a serious conflict, step in and encourage your kids to talk. Listen to them, separating them to calm down if the need arises. When there is hitting, stop it immediately and demand an apology. Make them understand that physical attacks aren't allowed. Use consequences like lost privileges, extra chores, or a time-out.

8. Bossy Behavior

Wouldn't it feel embarrassing if you heard people describing your kids as bossy? Even if this description isn't complimentary, it may not be far from the truth. If your child is the type that tells other kids what to do all the time, you should act fast.

Example 1:

A child with an assertive personality can cause conflict with friends and family members. Even though his behavior may indicate great future leadership skills, the behavior can appear bossy if extreme.

What to do:

- Listen to your child. Yes, you read that right! Despite being bossy, your child needs to be heard because they need to talk about why they were overly assertive. They may not intend to cause trouble, but it can be their way of making other kids follow the rules. By listening to them, you can teach them how to communicate their emotions in friendly and polite ways.
- Help them understand what empathy is all about. We already discussed what empathy means in the last chapter. Since your child may not know they are misbehaving, you can encourage them to be empathetic. Show them that they can think about other kids and how their actions and words can affect people. Let them know the impact of their actions and what happens if they keep behaving this way.

What not to do:

- Never call your child "bossy." You don't have to tell them their friends are avoiding them because it will affect their confidence. Instead, teach them that being strong-willed and assertive are great characteristics if they are expressed in the right way.

- Don't ignore your child's behavior, thinking that their overly assertive behavior will resolve on its own as they grow up. Remember that you are their role model and teacher. It's your duty to teach them what's right and wrong.
- Let them know that being bossy will hurt others, so the behavior needs to stop.

In conclusion, these eight strategies are only beneficial if put to good use. If you notice that your child continues misbehaving, you may need to speak to your doctor. Sometimes, children's misbehavior is a sign of an underlying health condition.

PART 4

NO MORE
ANGRY PARENT

CHAPTER 11

LESS ANGRY PARENTING CHECKLIST

"Self-care is not self-indulgence, it is self-preservation, and that is an act of political warfare."

— Audre Lorde

As parents, you have needs just as your kids do. For example, you need time to spend with your friends, you need time to engage in activities you enjoy, and above all, you need time to take care of yourself.

You may be wondering, *"What does taking care of yourself have to do with becoming a less angry parent?"* The truth is, as much as you love your kids, parenting can be very stressful. When you constantly experience high-stress levels, it's easy to become tense, impatient, and angry. This lifestyle can affect your eating and sleeping patterns. Ignoring self-care can lead to anxiety and depression, especially for parents without a support system. It helps to have support when you're experiencing worries about finances, divorce, or relocation.

Being a good parent for your child doesn't mean you need to sacrifice your needs so you can tend to your child's needs. Instead, it's about finding the perfect balance between your needs and your child's. Sometimes, simply taking a break from your child's needs to recharge your batteries works.

When your individual needs are met, you'll find it easier to stay calm in stressful situations. Managing your child's challenging behaviors becomes easier, and you'll find your patience levels grow. You can be present with them fully. If you take care of yourself, you can become calmer. Ultimately, to become a peaceful parent, you need to understand what self-care entails and then practice it.

Are your kids getting the best version of you, or do you just manage to be physically present? If your answer's the latter, it's time to explore what you can do to care for yourself better. In this chapter, we focus on ourselves and what we should do to become less angry individuals.

What Is Self-Care, Anyway?

Are you a parent that sees self-care as being self-indulgent? If so, now's the time to get that idea out of your head.

Self-care is **taking care** of your physical, social, and emotional needs. It involves nurturing your whole body while setting aside time to maintain your overall well-being. On the other hand, self-indulgence is when you do things you love or indulge in them **excessively.**

Many parents see self-care as self-indulgence, but that's a misconception. What comes to mind when these parents think of self-care is usually an image of themselves sunbathing, watching waves of water at the beach, or immersing themselves in a bubble bath and sipping champagne. Unfortunately, incorrect assumptions like these can discourage parents from practicing self-care, even though self-care, in its correct form, will improve their emotional and physical well-being.

The main difference between self-care and self-indulgence is the result. Practicing self-care results in staying healthy and being at the top of your game. The result of engaging in self-indulgence often becomes avoiding important tasks and wasting time binge-watching TV. We all know the latter won't bring real solutions to your anger.

But how can parents have time for themselves when they need to juggle grocery shopping, do laundry, bathe their kids, prepare meals, and otherwise keep up with their busy schedules? How can you squeeze time in for self-care when every day already feels like a battle to you?

Practicing self-care regularly will, over time, bring positive feelings. Self-indulgence will affect your health in the long run despite being fun at first.

It's not breaking news that parents tend to focus on their kids and hardly have time for themselves. Doing simple things such as soaking in a bath, styling your hair, and wearing attractive dresses and shoes may seem like hard work. Let alone creating time for other activities to improve your professional and social health. But don't forget that taking care of yourself daily means looking out for yourself and your loved ones.

Wondering how you can do this?

If you view self-care from the right lens, you can see that indulging in it isn't selfish, and doing it eventually helps your children and other people around you. When you have time for your needs and are well-rested, you can be more patient with your kids.

For example, when your toddler whines at 9:00 am, it won't feel so bad since you've slept well, had a hot cup of coffee, and even eaten a healthy, well-balanced breakfast. In this case, you have a higher patience level which helps you handle the stress of your child's meltdown more effectively. The tantrums won't feel overwhelming, and your day can go on smoothly.

Note that self-care won't make parenting easier overnight. It's not like waving a magic wand and everything becomes perfect immediately. However, practicing self-care can make it easier for you to cope with the challenges that come with parenting. Consider the popular saying that "you can't pour from an empty bucket." If you don't have energy left, how can you take care of others?

The Best Self-Care Checklist

To enact change and leave behind those self-neglecting tendencies, I've created a self-care checklist you can use as part of your self-care discovery journey.

1. Are You Getting Enough Sleep?

Parenting can be so overwhelming that getting a good night's sleep becomes less of a priority. Even though becoming a parent is one of the most wonderful things you can experience, it can impact your well-being and health, and even interfere with your sleep. Parents need to understand that sleep deprivation can cause:

- Anxiety
- Depression
- High blood pressure
- Obesity

- Decreased brain function
- Heart attacks

Sleep deprivation can also trigger and worsen symptoms of postpartum depression.

As a parent who wants to experience peaceful parenting, you sometimes need to schedule nap times. Naps help exhausted moms and dads rest. Adequate sleep is more important than picking up your kids' building blocks in the living room. Once in a while, let yourself forget that your house is a mess. Skip the little chores that day and get rest instead! This can't be overemphasized. If you're sick, you won't have the energy to do the chores anyway. So why not let those things be and get rest?

Getting the right amount of sleep will heal your body and mind, reduce fatigue, and re-energize you. You'll be able to handle the challenges of the day without feeling overwhelmed. Sometimes, it's as simple as stopping what you are doing and lying down. Catch extra sleep when your kids are sleeping. These nap times are also for you and not just for kids! Your kids will appreciate you more if you aren't cranky. Get your kids to bed early, and you should go to bed immediately after they do.

2. Are You Exercising?

What would happen to your whole family if you were burned out, tired, overwhelmed, frustrated, and angry? As the caregiver, your emotional and physical health indirectly affects everyone around you, so it's important that you practice self-care.

No doubt, creating the time and having the energy to exercise can seem daunting, especially when you have to cope with everyone's needs. But a simple 10 to 20 minutes of exercise daily will give you amazing benefits like boosting your mood and energy, improving your cognitive performance, protecting you against chronic diseases, improving your quality of sleep, boosting your self-confidence, and reducing feelings of anxiety and depression. Besides, exercising can be fun!

I used to feel so tired from being a "good" parent until I started getting up early in the morning to exercise. I wasn't doing this because I enjoyed doing planks or doing yoga at 6:00 am but because I knew that after I finished and had a shower, I would feel recharged. I'd feel more energized to get through the day ahead of me. The exercise got my blood flowing, and the shower would sweep away the worries I had from the day before.

This habit brought about a powerful change in my life. Suddenly, I could start my day filled with energy, power, patience, and less anger. I also realized that setting small exercise goals and ticking them off gave me a special feeling of pride.

Exercise also allows you to access a large support network where you connect with people socially. By taking dance classes, exercise classes such as yoga, tai chi, Pilates, and Zumba, or going to the gym, you can meet other people with the same fitness goals that you have.

3. Are You A Multitasker?

When you hear the word "multitasking," what comes to mind? Do you see yourself as a great multitasker because you can cook, clean, and do other house chores simultaneously? Well, what you are doing in that case isn't just multitasking but task-switching. By constantly tasking your brain to switch gears, you can easily get exhausted. You may find you barely accomplish anything at the end of the day.

Don't get me wrong. I'm not insinuating that multitasking is wrong. Of course, there are times when you *must* multitask. However, multitasking, if done constantly, can affect your parenting ability.

Balancing your career and household chores is a never-ending job. It involves running errands, cleaning the bathroom, preparing meals, and helping your kids with their homework. You aren't a machine, and multitasking can stress you out because you exhaust yourself by doing it all.

As I mentioned earlier, it's okay to leave your living room with your kid's toys on the floor while you focus on doing more pressing things. It's okay to order food for delivery a few times a week. You don't need to act like the greatest chef of all time. It's okay for your partner to help out with the laundry or other house chores when they return from work. You don't need to do everything by yourself.

Save your sanity by prioritizing and doing fewer chores if you can. Multitasking can affect your brain and your body, making you anxious and more likely to get triggered and yell at your kids.

Things to think about:

- What are the things causing you a significant amount of stress?
- What areas can you make changes in to give you more time and energy for parenting?
- What are the coping strategies you can use that will work for you?
- How can you simplify your life?

Be the best parent you can be by taking care of yourself mentally and physically. Rest and prioritize.

You can only do your best when you are at your best.

4. Are You A Good Teammate?

Since parenting can be very stressful, it's important to seek support. Don't allow it to be a one-person job. If you're always engaging in arguments with your partner and don't understand each other, it'll be difficult to make things work.

Parents tend to complain more, get worn out, irritated, and stressed out from all their daily tasks. If all the tasks are left for one person to do, it leads to more anxiety and frustration, creating an unhappy home environment.

Does this conversation below sound like your situation?

Mom: *"You're never here. You are hardly home. And when you are home, your mind isn't here. You don't help out at all!"*

Dad: *"You never appreciate what I do here."*

Mom: *"What? Then you also don't appreciate all my hard work either."*

Conversations like this can lead to heated arguments which won't get the work done or change the situation. To achieve peaceful parenting, one person shouldn't be left to do everything. Teamwork is a priority. If you have a good teammate who you love and understand, the chances for you to get angry will be reduced.

Ensure there is clear and consistent communication. If you want your partner to help out, don't assume that they know what to do. Instead, tell your partner what you'd like for them to do. For example, make a list of things that should be done (laundry, dishes, cleaning, cooking, bathing the child, grocery shopping, etc.) and who will do them.

If you and your partner have a good relationship, this shouldn't be hard. Prioritize the time you spend with each other. Even with the chaos, you still need to be there for each other.

Things to think about:

- Are you a supportive partner?
- Do you spend time with your partner in the evenings or on weekends?
- What is the tone of your voice when talking?
- Do you lose your cool or get angry towards your partner when they fail to do something you asked them to do?
- Do you think you are a good teammate?

You'll find that parenting becomes easier when you make time for yourself. Be mindful of your emotions and tend to your needs when you notice your energy level is low. Practicing self-care helps not just you but your entire family.

CHAPTER 12

LESS ANGRY PARENTING ROUTINE

"It is human to be angry, but childish to be controlled by anger."

— Mokokoma Mokhonoana

When dealing with anger, you have some options. Maybe you want to learn how to stop yourself from getting angry before it escalates. You may want to prevent your anger from becoming uncontrollable, or learn how to stay calm and simply be less angry. Fortunately, there are routines you can engage in to help you stay cool.

We all know that too much anger can be dangerous for your health. Intense emotions can be tough to deal with. Prevent these over-the-top feelings by starting your day off right with the less angry parenting routines shared in this chapter.

While I don't have all the answers to less angry parenting, I do know what has worked for me when raising a large family. One thing you should always have at the back of your mind is realizing that the only person you can control is you. Therefore, you need to be cool with yourself first to stay on top of this parenting game, regardless of what happens around you.

If you want to stop screaming and manage your anger better each day, you need to create healthy routines. These routines can help you and your kids maintain a positive mood and avoid getting triggered. These routines will set you up for success for the rest of your day!

Your Morning Routine

Have you heard of the saying, *"A good day starts with a good beginning"*? As simple as this may sound, it carries significance. Even though we fail to admit it, many of us know that our day usually goes smoother after experiencing a great morning.

Perhaps you already have a morning routine for you and your kids. Still, you keep getting pulled in different directions. The morning flies by, and you suddenly wonder why you got so tired despite not achieving much. Of course, this situation can make any parent feel anxious, affecting your mood for the rest of your day.

For this reason, how you start your day is critical. You need these routines to set the tone for the rest of your day. So, even though creating a mommy morning routine may seem impossible and overwhelming, it can be done. If I can do it, then you can, too.

Many parents share this struggle. Just a few minutes after a parent walks out of the bedroom, they see that their kids want breakfast, need a diaper change, prefer the other sibling's cup for their milk, are fighting with siblings, and can't find their school clothes.

No one wants to start their day like this, so what can you do? Here are some effective habits you can start now to make the rest of your day more peaceful.

1. Rest The Night Before

This is the first on the list because your "morning" routine should start the night before. If you don't go to bed early, how do you expect yourself to get up and be productive? For example, if you went to bed late at 3:00 am and had to be up by 7:00 am, there is no way you will have rested enough to start your day well. Your emotions will be all over the place, and just about anything can set you off.

We've already discussed why you need to rest in the last chapter. I can't overemphasize its importance. Rest the night before to be fully recharged for the new day.

2. Plan Out Your Next Day

It helps to have a plan for the next day. Map out what you will be doing the next day and follow through. A day without a plan is like fighting an uphill battle. The day passes by but you're still figuring out what you need to do.

Planning your morning (and the rest of the day) means budgeting your time properly. This step helps you avoid getting to the end of your day and realizing that you wasted your time. Likewise, when you plan the night before, you free up your brain for the next day.

Note that I am not saying you must follow a strict deadline without changes. Is that even possible with kids? (I doubt it.) Instead, be flexible. This is why we are discussing your routines and not your schedules. Routines are flexible. You need to figure out what you want to do the same way every day and what tasks change day to day.

3. Morning Mindset

Parenting can be overbearing, especially when our expectations aren't met. It becomes hard for us to have a positive attitude each day. Regardless, you need to keep in mind that a positive mindset helps adjust your focus and prepare you for the challenges of the day.

Positive affirmations can help set the tone of the day ahead of you. Here are a few of the positive affirmations I use and have found to be very helpful. You can read them aloud every morning before starting your day:

✓ *Today, I will be more patient with my kids.*
✓ *Today, I will love my kids more. I will not yell or scream.*
✓ *Today, I will do my best to focus on myself and not my kids. The problem is me and not my kids.*
✓ *Today, I will watch over my thoughts, behavior, and language.*
✓ *I can become a better mom/dad/parent, and I know I will.*
✓ *I know that yelling or screaming isn't a solution.*
✓ *I know I am raising a tiny beautiful human. I choose to live in the moment with my child.*

To help you set the right mindset, you can also consider putting limits on your social media time. My phone has this feature that allows me to turn off apps or mute them before a certain time of the day. For example, certain apps are disabled for the first 20 minutes of my day. Even though this timeframe seems short, it's enough to keep me from scrolling through Facebook or other social media first thing in the morning.

4. Get Dressed (No Sloppy Pajamas All Day)

This particular routine has been neglected by many moms even though basic hygiene and looking good were a priority before having a baby. Include, at the very least, a simple, basic hygiene routine in your morning routine, no matter what.

What does basic hygiene mean to you? For me, it includes showering, brushing my teeth, taking whatever supplements or medications I have, styling my hair, and dressing up.

The dressing up aspect is a big one for me because how you dress can affect your mood. According to Dr. Karen Pine in her 2021 University of Hertfordshire study, *"Clothing doesn't just influence others, it reflects and influences your mood."*

Some moms will get so comfortable ditching their sexy slit dresses, shorts, and high heels and always choose to wear baggy yoga pants, sweatshirts, and flip-flops. Don't get me wrong. I'm not suggesting that you shouldn't wear these items. I'm only advising that you dress intentionally for the day. If dressing in attractive outfits will make you feel and act your best, please dress that way! If you plan to take a walk with your kids or alone, dress for the occasion!

It's likely that at some point, your outfit has stopped you from doing something fun because you didn't want (or didn't have time) to change your clothes. So why not start your day **right** by wearing the **right** clothes? Think about your day before selecting your clothes.

5. Healthy Breakfast

Parents set the mood of the day for everyone. It's important to start the day right for everyone with a healthy and nutritious breakfast. While many of us know this tip, we don't always keep it in mind. During the morning rush, we choose unhealthy options like processed foods or even skip breakfast for convenience.

Even during those busy mornings, remember that the food you eat can affect how you function throughout the day. If you eat a small, sugary meal to start your day off, you'll find your energy levels plummeting as the day goes on. So ditch the donuts or leftover pizza and take the time to prepare something tasty that puts you in a good mood. A well-balanced meal can sustain you throughout the day while keeping your mood in check.

How you treat your body often determines how your kids will treat theirs too. Of course, there are some days when you don't feel like eating well for yourself. You just don't care. How about you do it for the beautiful little ones watching you? You'll be rewarded with your household's good mood.

Your Bedtime Routine

Your bedtime routine is also essential. When creating your bedtime routine, whether as a stay-at-home or working parent, ensure that it's flexible and reasonable. Keep it simple. This isn't a schedule but a routine.

Here is an example of how to set your bedtime routine:

- ✓ **8:00 – 8:30 pm:** Kids should be brushing their teeth, bathing, changing into their pajamas, listening to a bedtime story for 10-20 minutes, and then it lights out (depending on their age).
- ✓ **8:30 pm:** Parents can watch or listen to something relaxing while sipping on a cup of tea or scrolling through social media. This can be done for 30 minutes to 1 hour, depending on the mood.
- ✓ **9:00 pm:** It's time for some self-care! Parents can go through their nighttime skincare routine, brush their teeth, and enjoy a nice long bath.
- ✓ **9:30 pm:** Parents retire to bed and have about 30 minutes to chat with their partner or read a book.
- ✓ **10:00 pm:** This is the time to rest, sleep, and recharge for the next morning!

Despite having the same amount of hours every day, a night routine can make you feel more energized, organized, less anxious, and happier. That's good for everyone! If you follow a routine, you'll have time for tasks without yelling at your kids. Ensure you are consistent with your routine. Make your kids follow through, and they will get used to it over time.

Whenever you feel like deviating, remind yourself why you have a routine–to manage your emotions better. You won't have to yell or scream at your child.

Parenting Quotes for Hard Times

Here, I share powerful parenting quotes. These are surefire ways to get you through tough times and alleviate the stress of parenting. They'll help keep your anger at bay and allow you to enjoy raising your little one.

When Your Child Is Pushing The Boundaries

Knowing what to do when your child constantly pushes boundaries is hard. It requires patience, but it will get better. However, if you feel like you're in the midst of a never-ending battle, the following quotes can reassure you:

- ✓ *"If you have never been hated by your children you haven't been a parent."* – Bette Davis.
- ✓ *"Any child in his right mind will test the limits. That's his job. He's pretty new on the planet, after all, and he's figuring out the rules. The most common reason that children test the limits is that they really want to find out where those limits are."* – Dr. Laura Markham.

When You Feel You Have Lost Your Way

Sometimes, you will feel stuck, constantly experiencing bad days. You may feel like you aren't creating the best lifestyle for yourself and your kids. Maybe you don't know how to get out of this rut or start over. The quotes below teach valuable lessons when you feel overwhelmed. They encourage you to take the first step, even if it's very small.

- ✓ *"If you can't fly, run. If you can't run, walk. If you can't walk, crawl, but by all means, keep moving."* – Martin Luther King Jr.
- ✓ *"The man who moves a mountain begins by carrying away small stones."* – Confucius.
- ✓ *"If you are stuck in a rut, do something different. Just pick one small thing."* – Dr. Lucy Russell.
- ✓ *"Don't let the muggles get you down."* – J.K. Rowling.
- ✓ *"Do what you can, with what you've got, where you are."* – Theodore Roosevelt.

When You Feel Overwhelmed

As parents, you sometimes find yourself wrapped up in the small daily tasks of being a parent and forget the bigger picture. The following quotes will remind you of the "why" behind parenting.

- ✓ *"Let your children live as children. They're only that little for a short while!"* – Unknown.
- ✓ *"We get frustrated at our children, but only until they grow up and leave the house."* – Michael Stutman.
- ✓ *"The kids who need the most love will ask for it in the most unloving ways."* –Russell Barkley.
- ✓ *"Remember you are not managing an inconvenience. You are raising a human being."* – Kittie Franz.

✓ *"A baby will make love stronger, days shorter, nights longer, bankroll smaller, home happier, clothes shabbier, the past forgotten, and the future worth living for."* – Pablo Picasso.

✓ *"Have patience. All things are difficult before they become easy."* – Saadi.

When they get caught up with their daily tasks, many parents often forget that kids grow up fast and are only young for a limited period. Make sure you cherish every moment you have with them. Think about how you want your child to remember you and act accordingly.

Your kids are watching you, and they want to be like you–they look up to you. The routines you set for yourself are good for both your body and your mind. They will put you in a good mood and keep anger at bay, making intense feelings more manageable.

CONCLUSION

Well done!

You've reached the end of this life-changing journey, and I must applaud you for staying with me until the end. I hope the journey has been as exciting for you as it was for me. But before I leave, I have a few words for you.

No doubt, parenting can be very challenging for every parent. Kids may act unpredictable, moody, and reckless, which results in parents struggling with their own anger issues. If you find yourself in this kind of situation, know that you aren't alone. Many moms and dads also struggle with anger issues.

The idea that some of your friends struggle with parenting their kids may seem absurd to you because you've always admired the kind of bond your friends share with their kids. You've probably wished it was that easy for you. But, the truth is, everyone will always put on their best face when they are in public with their kids. It's an entirely different situation when they are back at home. Emotions may become overwhelming when they don't need to put on a happy face for others.

Even the most loving and patient parents still struggle with getting a grip on their emotions and keeping their cool. So cheer up! You don't need to beat yourself over it, especially when you have the way out now. Although the feeling isn't a great one, it's the same for many parents out there.

Dealing with anger issues isn't easy, even though I wish it were. The bad emotions that come with it can make us feel like a monster, especially when we feel guilty about how we treated our kids.

This book has discussed different strategies for dealing with anger and how to keep your cool. To learn how to deal with anger, you need to first accept that you can be an angry parent. Everyone has the potential. You also need to focus on changing yourself and not the kids. You are the problem, not them!

We also need to understand that despite anger being an emotion that we all feel, it negatively affects our kids when we express it in the wrong ways. Many parents aren't aware that their anger can so negatively affect their kids, but it does. Communicating or correcting your child doesn't require yelling, spanking, or any anger at all.

I understand that parenting is difficult for you, and you are going through difficult times as you cope with your emotions and your kids. However, yelling and putting your kid down will only exhaust you, making it harder to cope with the issues you face. Instead of labeling yourself with negative words, start welcoming positive words into your life. You will eventually see that you are a great parent and there is room for change.

Being an angry parent doesn't define who you are. There is still time to change. Even if you've made mistakes and done things you regret, you can put the past behind you by making things right. Consider apologizing to those affected by your actions and use what you've learned so far to put your actions in check.

Whenever you feel intense emotions, stop and reflect on the last incident that made you angry. Consider how you could've handled the situation differently. Then, think of what you can do now to change how you react in the future. Your today doesn't have to be like yesterday. Every day is a new opportunity.

As you continue being a loving parent to your little one, remember that no parent is perfect. Everyone makes mistakes. Kids don't need heroes. They need loving parents to guide and support them whenever they need it. You don't need to care about how everyone around you is doing it. Focus on yourself!

The road ahead may be a bit rough. Expect challenges, but the journey will be worth it. With your new knowledge, you can identify ways to manage your feelings and find more happiness and peace in your home.

Enjoy the journey!

leave a review

I'm truly delighted that you read my book. I hope it helps as a fellow parent. Your review will mean the world to me and keep me on my journey to help others.

Thank you for your help.

Carrie Khang

SCAN ME

REFERENCES

What are parenting triggers? (2021, march). Retrieved from https://www.todaysparent.com/family/parenting/parenting-triggers/

Dr. Paul Jenkins. (2020, July). How to Stop Yelling at Your Kids. Retrieved from https://www.youtube.com/watch?v=YMXrdTwRdZs&t=91s

Hal Edward Runkel, Scremfree Parenting (n.d). Parenting is not about Kids, it's about parents.

Glembocki, V. (2022, January). How to Stop Yelling at Your Kids—and What to Do Instead. Retrieved from https://www.parents.com/parenting/better-parenting/advice/how-to-quit-yelling-at-your-kids/

Li, P. (2022, October). Discipline vs Punishment: The Difference In Child Development. Retrieved from https://www.parentingforbrain.com/discipline-vs-punishment/

Morin, A. (2021, January). Role Model the Behavior You Want to See From Your Kids. Retrieved from https://www.verywellfamily.com/role-model-the-behavior-you-want-to-see-from-your-kids-1094785

Li, P. (2022, October). How To Get Kids To Listen. Retrieved from https://www.parentingforbrain.com/how-to-get-kids-to-listen/

Yasser Abdelazim Abdelmawgoud Samak. (2016, September) What happens when you're an angry parent? Retrieved from https://valley-international.net/index.php/theijsshi/article/view/568

Nancy A. Brown. (n.d). Why do children misbehave? Retrieved from http://denton.agrilife.org/files/2011/09/behaviorproblemsinchildren_1.pdf

Lindsey Roberts. (2017, January). Why self-care is important? Retrieved from https://www.washingtonpost.com/lifestyle/on-parenting/in-defense-of-a-parents-day-off/2017/01/23/270ffafc-d8f2-11e6-b8b2-cb5164beba6b_story.html

Printed in Great Britain
by Amazon

29416968R00085